One Nation Under God

Written by:
Dr. T. K. Harvey-Allen

Cadmus Publishing
www.cadmuspublishing.com

Copyright © 2021 Dr. T. K. Harvey-Allen

Published by Cadmus Publishing
www.cadmuspublishing.com
Port Angeles, WA

ISBN: 978-1-63751-140-4

All rights reserved. Copyright under Berne Copyright Convention, Universal Copyright Convention, and Pan-American Copyright Convention. No part of this book may be reproduced, stored in a retrieval system, or transmitted in any form, or by any means, electronic, mechanical, photocopying, recording or otherwise, without prior permission of the author.

ACKNOWLEDGEMENTS

    Giving honor to God, to whom is the only true religion. I recognize at this time during the writing of this book all of the individuals that are and have impacted my life thus far and for those familiar allies that have stayed the course through many storms and turbulence that I have passed through. I would like to take this time out to both acknowledge and recognize one of the most realist guys on planet Earth, Mr. Bailey Conard. When things imploded you proved your worth, and when disloyalty and betrayal were at an all-time high you gave a new meaning to "real." Thank you, 1,000,000 times over for being you. Trust me, I'll forever be grateful. Loyalty comes from on the inside of us more times than not. It is dictated by emotions, and love is an action word. I acknowledge the dream team over at PGC, Inc. I thank you all for your individual contributions and for your helpful insights to making us a better team. God allows us all to fall down at times. For some of us, many times. Falling down isn't the measuring stick of the obvious but finding ways to get up is. I appreciate my friend Joseph "Southwest" Guyton for his talented contribution to the cover illustration for this book cover and for listening to various excerpts from this book as I created it. Lastly, to Kevin "Tricky" Edwards and my brother in all things Alexius "Nephew" Nelson. Thanks to these guys for being my sounding boards and for being men of character and substance, and to Mrs. Heidi Conard for her patience and loyalty, you were A-1 from day one.

"The secret to failure is trying to please everyone."

DEDICATIONS

This book is dedicated to Positive Growth Consulting, Incorporated (PGC, Inc.). I love you guys. To my parents, Mr. and Mrs. Johnny Allen, I apologize if I've ever let you down. I do, however, respect the fact that you all always allowed me to be me. Finally, to Donald "Dun G" Wynne: RIP kid.

This book is dedicated to the African American people who died in the senseless murder of the 1921 Tulsa Massacre of 300 African American men, women, and children. This book is also dedicated to the African American people of the Houston Riots of 1917, which was one of the most tragic chapters of the Jim Crow era, dubbed, "The largest murder trial in the history of the United States," also known as the Logan Camp Mutiny. To all of the people who have lost and sacrificed their lives to the system of oppression, hate, and racism. We as descendants must recognize that death isn't the end of a journey; for even in death your pain is felt and your voices from the grave are heard. It is in your sacrifices that continues to motivate a movement.

Contents

PART 1 1

PART 2 55

PART 3 77

ABOUT THE AUTHOR 96

DR. T. K. HARVEY-ALLEN

PART 1

I CAN'T BREATHE

May 2020 George Floyd's death ignited a multi-racial movement never seen before in the history of America: In May 2020 the police in Minneapolis, Minnesota apprehended an African American male by the name of George Floyd. As they attempted to arrest, subdue, and contain Mr. Floyd they held him down pinned to the ground with knees on his back and head as they held him in a (now outlawed) chokehold. Mr. Floyd, barely audible, got out of his voice box, "I can't breathe," yet the police officers of the Minneapolis Police Department continued their brutal assault of George Floyd. Finally, after eight minutes and forty-six seconds, George Floyd died by the hands of the Minneapolis Police Department.

Police is defined as an organized civil force for maintaining order, preventing and detecting crime, and enforcing the laws.

In a civilized country and/or state the police are a necessity. Law and order are what makes a state civilized. Without the enforcement of rules and/or laws set forth by government there would be no order, there would only be chaos and mayhem. Thus, if the police who are supposed to enforce these rules (which should be based on ethics, morals, and standards that exhibit peace, discipline, and control) do not abide by these ethical, moralistic, and standardized rules, if the guardians of the state go against the very fiber of what they are supposed to represent, then all the faith and trust we have as a nation have been defiled and breached. The rule of order is what our universe is created on. One can surmise that humankind has copied God's pattern of rule. There is an authority (the government) that the people answer to and hold accountability to with the ultimate judge being the infinite God Himself and the ultimate rulebook being the Holy Bible. The rules of a land as they are given to a people to obey, abide, and structure their lives around is called law. Laws are a system of rules established by a government or an authority to which they are applied to humankind (more on the law and laws later in the book). God is the sovereign authority who dictates and commands all simply because He created all; therefore, when rules and laws are violated, we subjects under these laws must be disciplined according to the penalties that are holding these laws in place. God said, "The wages of sin is death" (Rom. 6:23). At times people attempt to be technical when it comes to try and prove a point, so some may say that statement by Paul wasn't a law, nor was it a commandment from God. The Bible, and every word that it contains, isn't just about God.

For the Bible is the vox dei (the voice of God). Every scripture is God breathed. When human beings that are acting in the capacity of guardians of the law or of those that are entrusted to enforce the law without biased tendencies, violate the trust of the people to which the law directly applies, civil unrest occurs simply because government and those that enforce governmental rule are held to a standard. After all, why would someone pledge allegiance to rule and enforce those rules but don't themselves believe in the rules or laws that they are enforcing?

Houston, TX 2019 the Houston Police Department's (HPD) narcotics division obtained a "No Knock Warrant" for a residence occupied by a Caucasian couple, Regina Nichols and her husband Mark. It was initially reported by the HPD and the media that the residence in which the husband and wife both occupied together was an infamous "drug house" (a home used to sell drugs). The police kicked in the door and murdered Regina and her husband. The police found no drugs, at least not enough to substantiate a "No Knock Warrant." It was determined in the aftermath of the extinguishing of innocent lives through an investigation by the HPD's internal affairs division that: A) the residence in which the couple resided was in fact not a reported "drug house"; B) the officers involved, in which the main primary conspirator is an African American, used false evidence to obtain the warrant in question; and C) the police raided the wrong house. Both federal and state criminal felony charges have been filed during the writing of this book; no legal conclusion or remedy has been established, instituted, or finalized.

Police of different nationalities raided the home of these citizens with a legal warrant obtained by illegal means (lies and deception). There wasn't an aggressive protest by the citizens of Houston or anywhere. Why? Do white lives matter? I believe that under the one God of everyone that all lives matter. Black lives matter is the absolute rallying cry, the subject matter, and the slogan of this era's reality when by a considerable margin only black folks are getting murdered in the name of justice (pronounced "just us").

People of every color, nationality, and creed didn't turn out in droves because of the senseless murders of these people by the police because, I believe, the HPD swiftly put a Band-Aid over the problem, temporarily stopping the bleeding (the public outcry), then as swiftly they cut the infected part off (the officers involved). The police department, at a minimum, suffered public embarrassment and humiliation. In government a lot of times it isn't about political ideology nor is it about political agenda, but it is about how a situation that has nuclear implications is handled by the folks in charge. We have to remember that when sensitive issues and situations arise that because of a very diverse world that we live in we as humankind are going to have conflicting opinions, thus producing conflicting beliefs, which in turn breeds various remedies on how these things should be resolved or tended to.

George Floyd became a universal martyr with his dying last words of, "I can't breathe," after all of the instances of racial injustice that has both occurred and taken place after similar tragedies had already taken place in other cities and towns throughout the United States. after a police officer in Dallas, TX wandered into the wrong apartment and killed an innocent man in his own residence. After a young lady was brutally arrested in Montgomery County, TX for a traffic violation and ended up dead in the county jail.

We may ask ourselves, "Why now?" Why this particular incident? In this horrific tragedy we can see more clearly the reasons for protest and see George Floyd's senseless murder wasn't what got us to this point. Emmett Till, Trayvon Martin, Dr. Martin Luther King Jr., Breonna Taylor, Rayshard Brooks, the Nichols couple, those and many more not named have gotten us to this point. One thing for certain, I call it the "Slow Drip Theory," we can put a garden hose in a bucket and turn on the water to a slow, steady drip. If we allow that dripping of water to continue to drip into that bucket, never turning the water off, at one point the bucket is going to overflow and spill out all over the place. George Floyd's death is the product of not turning the water off. Social injustices, inequality, racial prejudices, racial profiling by the American justice system, and the county and city police departments all around the United States turned that water on long ago. The district attorneys all across the country passively sat by and just watched every drip of water slowly drip into that bucket drip by horrific drip and did nothing until that final drip came, and the bucket of police brutality, police injustice, the bucket of corrupt political machines in cities and towns trademark, courtrooms of justice (pronounced "just us"), where the lawlessness of the law is forced upon the poverty-stricken ghettos and barrios, the bucket of greed and political ambitions that supersedes what is morally right, caring not the destruction that it has caused, has finally overflowed.

What is so sad about all of these things is that wrongdoing and injustice has been very consistent in the poor Hispanic communities and poor Black communities for so long that things police do that are subject to question and suspect became the norm; therefore, no one says anything. The police in many neighborhoods across the country have failed those communities simply because of the mindset of the police that patrol these neighborhoods have given the examples by actions and voices that they can do as they please, to whomever they please, when they please. The normal that is evidenced consists of control, subdue, arrest, harass, do harm, and increasingly becoming popular these days, to kill. Am I advocating that all police are bad cops or even bad human beings? ABSOLUTELY NOT. What I am saying, though, is that because we represent the same job, union, color, took the same oath, pledge, and swore to be brothers and sisters of the same order does not mean that if you or I commit an unethical, immoral action against another person's right to life, justice, and general way of being, that we should not have to answer for our wrongs. What I am saying is that if a fellow officer does something that he or she shouldn't, it doesn't matter about their uniform because the stark reality of it all is we are all human beings first, certainly not above God's law. Wrong is wrong, evil intent is evil intent, injustice is injustice, and racial bias is exactly what it is, racial bias. It doesn't matter who is doing it or participating in it.

Our society is weird at times. Certain success, likewise, certain failures, get overlooked many times depending on social status. The Saduces in the Bible were such folks. They felt that their persey "stuff didn't stink," but Jesus put them in their place. They were an aristocratic group in Israel that dominated the higher echelons of the priesthood. As land owners, they achieved the majority of their power and status from their class and positions as priests (Matt. 22:23-33).

It was reported that certain police officers called in and didn't show up for work in Atlanta, Georgia in protest of the officer getting charges brought against him for shooting Rayshard Brooks in the back twice, killing him. There is an old saying that applies to that incident: birds of a feather, flock together. Apparently, a heck of a lot of police there in Atlanta feel that it was okay to murder someone. I mean, due process is in fact a constitutional right of any American citizen. Likewise, it is a right to be charged and prosecuted when the law is broken. Being a police officer doesn't exempt anyone from prosecution when the law is broken and/or violated, thus, it is clearly apparent the mindset and mentality of many officers in the Atlanta Police Department.

It is extremely difficult to enforce the law without prejudice and impartiality when one does not in fact truly believe in what they are enforcing. The most memorable news piece came on the television the other night that made me speechless. All I could do was shake my head in sadness as I lay witness to a news clip of a police officer walking down the street alongside his other constituents. Along the police officer's route lined on both sides of the street were people of all races. I believe that they were in peaceful protest. Well, as the police walked, one officer spotted a small African American child. It was a little girl of no more than four years of age, I suppose, but the officer knelt down to the little girl as to give her a hug. As he reached out to embrace the child she asked the officer, "You aren't going to shoot me, are you?" I was stunned, to say the least!

This is the norm in most African American households and communities. We used to frighten young kids when they were being difficult or misbehaving. "Ima call the police." The police in the poverty-stricken neighborhoods, ghetto communities, and barrios are equivalent to the Boogeyman. Why? Because all that these children have both seen with their own eyes and heard with their own ears is the physical assaults, murder, mayhem, and chaos that the police bring when they show up. Many of these kids sat by and watched maybe a loved one being assaulted or carted off to jail. Protection isn't what these children feel when they see these types of occurrences, but fear of the police takes shape and forms the belief system that the cops are the enemy.

I truly believe that in order to solve any problem one has to be able to identify with that problem first in order to be effective within a problem-solving solution. Meaning that, if an individual is an alcoholic or a drug addict, who better to talk and counsel them than former alcoholics and/or drug addicts? I feel that it is great to get degrees and further our education, especially in our professions of choice. These degrees, certifications, and educational doctrines give us expertise and authority to talk about and teach about these things from a clinical, therapeutic, text, and observational perspective. In retrospect, I ask two distinct but fair questions: How can someone feel my pain if they've never hurt like me before? How can someone relate with my Blackness if they've never been Black?

Yes, people have empathy, but how can I put myself in someone else's shoes if I can't wear that person's shoe size? I feel that some people sympathize with a struggle or cause for various reasons. One of them is that they have witnessed up close the struggles of others and the heartache, pain, and inequality that it projects is repulsive, to say the least. Therefore, they unite with what they feel is right. I feel that some people, on the other hand, are just peaceful people and want peace. They want "no smoke," thus, they are angry at the ones causing it. I believe that society's way of thinking has evolved and changed as every drip hit on the inside of that bucket. Time kept changing and moving forward. As the hands of time ticked and tocked, so did the thinking of society. Examples of the evolution in humankind's progress is before us each waking moment of our New Millennial lives. Cell phones, internet, digital television, virtual reality, to name a few, are but a touch away at our disposition. The new ways of thinking are the reasons why there were multi-racial protests, both passive and aggressive, when that one drip of water (George Floyd's death) hit the bucket (racial injustice) that was already filled to the rim. It all came flowing over the edges simply because it couldn't hold any more water (police brutality, racial injustices, social injustices, cold-blooded murder of people of color by police). People of every color are saying loud and clear that this is no longer the 1960s, this isn't pre- nor post-Civil War, this is not the Jim Crow era, but this is one nation, united under one God, that this is the era of folk that refuse to be second class citizens to anyone.

In the late '70s and early '80s Hollywood rolled out to the African American communities non-stereotypical families, I suppose to give us role models and maybe entertainment that made us laugh. I once heard that sometimes we must laugh just to keep from crying. All in all, these were make-believe families that we could only fantasize in being like one day. "The Jeffersons" was one of them with George Jefferson owning dry cleaning businesses and living in a penthouse. I personally didn't know many African American during that time owning several businesses at one time living in penthouses complete with a doorman and a maid. The show was entertaining, though. Then came "The Cosbys." We all in the hood wanted those dreams for real. Of course, there were a few African Americans like Bob Johnson who was one of the first that I can remember (that I paid attention to) that was worth multimillions of dollars and wasn't an athlete, rapper, entertainer, or movie star.

Then in 2008 the glass ceiling was shattered by President Barack H. Obama. Kids' mentalities changed, grownups' mentalities changed. The dream all of the sudden became real. The most powerful man in the world was an African American. Martin Luther King Jr.'s dream had become a reality. African American kids didn't just aspire to be like Mike anymore. They were singing and dancing in the streets all over the world, especially here in the good ol' USA, to be like Barack! It was like one of those "where were you" moments. I remember watching television when President Obama was elected and watching people of color take to the streets celebrating. I also remember watching people crying in joy. I suppose that one of the most memorable moments of that night was watching a 93-year-old African American woman on television in tears saying that she never thought in her lifetime that she would live to see nor witness a Black man become President of the United States.

I didn't agree with all of President Obama's policies. However, I did respect, number one, him as an African American man who had accomplished what for a long time was seemingly impossible. President Obama not once stepped outside of the realm of being presidential. President Obama has class. As we call it in the neighborhood, President Obama has "sauce" (style). His wife, former First Lady Michelle Obama, was the first African American First Lady, who by her appearance commanded grace, intelligence, and she had her own "sauce" as well.

This was the first real-life family of husband, wife, and kids that we all paid attention to on the television simply because they were real. We didn't have to wait once a week to watch an episode on TV. These people were in our living rooms every single day. The Obamas were the dream that turned into actual reality. We could identify with not just the color of their skin, but we could identify with the color of their souls. These were genuine folks that gave a nation dreams that we didn't have to go to sleep to accomplish. "Yes, we can."

The way we think has evolved because of these people in accomplishment, success, and the impossible. We learned that the impossible is always possible. I have often believed in the phrase, "If you change the way you think, you will change your life." The way that we think and perceive things has a lot to do with many things. In saying that no one is born prejudiced or biased, somewhere along the way they had to be conditioned to hate, either from a traumatic experience or because they may have been taught this way by someone that they trust and believe in. The most wonderful thing about being in that state of being conditions is a mind can always be reprogrammed (John 15:12). The ticking tock of life's clock has shown us that the New Millennial thinking is the norm now and it's pushing and continues to push old, tired, outdated thinking, ideas, and traditional ways of problem-solving over a steep cliff.

One day I was walking and passed by a table consisting of white and Hispanic guys rapping and singing to a song. As I continued to observe, they each took turns in giving their own individual solo verse in rap form in the particular song with one of them banging out a beat with his fist on top of the table. These young men made me stop and pause for a couple of reasons. One reason that I paused was that there stood six young men, all of them non-African Americans, banging on the table in the middle of nowhere singing rap lyrics (it was obvious they rapped original material), and it actually sounded good. But what really piqued my interest was the lyrical substance of what they were rapping about. These young men were rapping about incarceration, poverty, violence, drugs, addiction, single mothers raising them, crime, money, sex, and death. These guys were telling their autobiographies through their flow of lyrics. In that moment it not only gave me pause in the way that I view certain things in the way of cultures, but that moment gave me new insight on the reconditioning of stereotypical norms. I then realized that these people and people of similar lifestyles are the young people of today's society. Maybe not in identical substance and circumstance, but they all share in a different unity, a different harmony. They identify with one another's struggles through the window of the things that they ENJOY. This is the thing that bonds this era of folks. They were all standing there rapping not because they expected to land a big music contract in the middle of nowhere. They were all doing the same thing at the same time because they all enjoyed doing what they were doing. In a sense, these people were representing the men, women, boys, and girls of the new struggle. The old struggle of equal education, equal employment, sitting at the back of the bus, having to enter a place of business through the back door, interracial marriage, drinking out of the same water fountain, all of those things represented a struggle that has taken on new issues and old struggles that have new faces.

 In the struggles of old we had to be careful in what we marched against. In this era the sky is the limit. Nothing short of total equality in all things is acceptable. In saying most miss the nucleus of the protests across America, the protest against the slow drip that was turned on long ago wasn't solely about racism because in part folks from every race, every nationality, and from all walks of life turned out in the thousands. Subsequently, the theme wasn't about a race of people as it amounted to the will of a people, and these people represented the society of Now. It was about familiarity, meaning the multiracial protests were about individuals that identified with one another because in THIS LIFE they live in the same neighborhoods, they work at the same jobs getting the same pay, they patronize the same food stores and convenience stores, the same clothing stores. They attend the same houses of worship, the same flea markets, the same bingo halls, the same institutions of higher learning, the same gas stations, and the same clinics. These protests in 2020 were about people with race a small factor, creed obsolete, and color semi-important, but these protests of 2020 were about folks of familiarity being opposed to the same tired, worn-out, outdated system of separatism that keeps insisting on being relevant within a society of indifference to the color of one's skin and social status. This millennial of diversity has created like-minded folk with like-minded interests that enjoy the same music, food, conversations. Furthermore, this millennial has created a culture like no other. Multiracial protest is the new voice of the new society that doesn't agree with injustice.

 I will take this moment to give credit where credit is due. The old Civil Rights Movement that included people like Dr. Martin Luther King Jr., Andrew Young, Rev. Al Sharpton, and Rev. Jessie Jackson did set the tide in motion. They set the examples of if you don't like your present conditions, change them. Change them through appeal in the way of solidarity in peaceful protest, in letting the system of oppression know that unfair treatment isn't acceptable.

Just like all things in life, that too has evolved. I believe that the protest of the '60s got their intended results to a certain degree. Though costing the life of Dr. King Jr. in the process, those protests in the '60s produced end results that merited change in several ways that the United States and the racist culture allowed to change. In analyzing that era during those times, one has to know that everyone at that time thought the same things about Black folks, so guess what that meant? Exactly. Everyone believed the same things as well. The backwoods thinking of a majority of the country, especially in the Deep South, was that they (the police) who then enforced the rules of the state, which were supposed to be comprised by the voices of society, could do no wrong.

When we vote and elect individuals to public office, we are literally giving them our individual seal of approval. We are saying with our vote that this person speaks for me. Making sense says that if a person speaks for another that they are definitely like-minded in ideology, philosophy, and ethical beliefs. So, if a candidate has been caught red-handed violating a rule or a principle and we yet vote for that person, that is indicative that we in turn support whatever it is that they did to raise questions. Remember that like-minded people support the same like-minded actions and agendas (Prov. 23:7).

In the era of the 1960s, peaceful protest was met with a resistance movement of its own, appropriately called the police department. They dealt with a peaceful movement with combative actions not because the protestors were in any way aggressive, violent, or militant in a physical manner, but because the movement by the police in the '60s was what I refer to as the "I dare you" movement. I dare you (Black man,

Black woman) to go against the very institution of slavery and oppression that has allowed you (Negro) to go free from picking cotton and calling me Master being put in chains, hung from trees, whipped, and beaten. I dare you to even act like you have a semblance of intelligence, to even suggest that you want to be equal, or the absurd suggestion that you want to live the same life of freedom and privilege that are only entitled to white folks. I dare you to want an education. You were not created to be smart, you were created to obey and serve. We, the people in the United States Constitution, did not include Black folks. They were slaves. Slaves were not considered people, they were considered property.

The fact of the matter is that the very system of slavery, oppression, and racism was shaken to its very core when the property of the '60s rebelled. See, this is where we get things "twisted" (wrong), meaning that it did not matter to the "I dare you" movement that these slaves, this property, did dare to oppose the very authority (the slave massa) that allowed them to exist in the first place. See, the system was not accustomed to slaves and property having a voice of any kind except to obey and comply. These protests (sound familiar?) were looked at as uprising, like slave revolts or slave rebellions of the 1800s, therefore, the system dealt with these revolts harshly by aggressive and militant actions in the way of water hoses, dogs, lynchings, and cold-blooded murder.

The system in the South had coexisted with another movement of enforcement then as well who had been around for quite some time. As a statement of fact, some of the policemen both belonged to and were active members of a fraternal order called the Ku Klux Klan, formed in 1866, whose primary functions were to deal with anyone that was considered a threat or opposed the institution of white supremacy. No, they were not legally employed by the citizens of this country. However, they worked their business of hate, bigotry, and murder nonstop without limitation.

Drip…drip…drip.

George Floyd's death was a direct byproduct of the thinking of the 1960s. A right to peaceful protest is a right that we all have as American citizens. It seems as though that right is only accepted and recognized if it doesn't go against public popular opinion and/or beliefs of others that feel like their own personal cause or agendas against human life. And basic human rights don't have to be per se "checked at the door." When other ways of thinking and viewing these things are opposite of our own, instead of weighing it all out to see really if someone is making sense, we automatically feel that our own thinking and ideas are in danger. Therefore, we do all that we can possibly do to prove our point, idea, or opinion. Most of the time it hasn't anything to do with right or wrong but everything to do with intent.

More times than not politicians by way of and through the media try and roll out certain African Americans (you know who they are) to take center stage out in the front of us by any and all media outlets that they possibly can. In this era there are plenty. Unlike the old days of just radio then television, there are a plethora of ways to reach the American public nowadays. This is truly the technology era and information age. Everything is literally at the tips of our fingers. When there is civil unrest of any kind they roll these people out in the front of us to tell us how we should feel and how we should think. Again, people haven't realized that the tools that used to fix certain issues and problems cannot be used to fix these problems any longer.

See, we can't solve the same problems (racism and social injustice) with the same tools. We must understand that, as the times evolve, so do the solutions. We must know that although the same problems and issues keep presenting themselves over and over again, there are different perpetrators involved. So, in essence the thinking is the same only in theory, not in substance. The police aren't the same police of yesteryear, so when these African American people are put in the front of us in the media platform of court jesters, it is an insult to the very fabric of why we are protesting in the first place.

How can a person tell an intelligent species how to think and what to feel about something that they can see with their own two eyes and hear with their own ears? We know that based on those two things alone that a belief system can be formed. Once someone sees something for themselves and hears something for themselves an opinion and belief takes place. To put someone on a media platform to tell a people that what they saw and what they heard was not actually what they both saw and heard is almost as bad as the actual injustice itself.

Destructive manipulation is what it is called, and we've watched it happen over and over again throughout the decades. These same African American people that they put on TV remind me of the African slave hunters that were used to hunt down men, women, boys, and girls in ancient Africa to capture them and sell them to the white slave traders so that they could bring them to America in chains (everyone that is your color, isn't you kind?).

See, the mentality once upon a time was that we could trust and depend on folks that looked like us and talked like us.

As time evolved the system figured out that any movement by a race of people had to have leaders in the midst that the others admired and looked at as leaders. The system allowed them to advance in education and so forth, creating status amongst their peers, even more so a trust and faith in those folks as representatives and examples for them on how the world should be viewed civilly through all of their eyes as a people. These people became the community, government, and political leaders.

What the system failed to do was change its theme (maybe it couldn't). Racism and social injustice have remained its main political theme. Point is that it has come disguised in many ways over the decades, and it has been championed by many African American politicians both directly and indirectly. The sad thing is that we have trusted many of these people as staples of our communities for a very long time. Some have been caught up in the legal bribery of what is called lobbying.

Are all African American politicians not good for us? Not what I'm saying. I am saying that everyone that looks the same are at many times not viewing life through the same telescope of life. I feel that in this era that we aren't as quick to trust folks that look like us, talk like us, and walk like us. We in this millennial more times than not tend to put our trust in those that think like us and feel like us.

Bottom line is that we trust those that trust us back. We believe in those that believe in us. A lot of times when a politician needs the Black vote they always seem to find their way to an African American big church somewhere. To me that is, and should be, the first red flag of destructive manipulation. I mean, during a nonelection year how many times did that politician appear at that church? See, this insult to our intelligence can't be, and by far isn't, ignored. These politicians do this as if it is normal. A lot of this foolishness has transpired simply because we've allowed it to go on for so long.

Multi-racial protest is a unified voice against all of the things very systematically wrong with everything that is going on (racial and social injustice). My biggest question, I would suppose, is that we've turned out to protest these wrongs and worn-out traditions of the old America, but will we turn out to the polls in the same force and numbers to vote for not who looks like us, for not who talks like us, but for who feels like we feel, for who thinks like we think, and who can relate to a changing of society's views of this day and time? This is the man or woman that we should want to be our voice within our city governments and our county, state, and national levels as well.

I figured out something awhile back and it has stuck with me for quite some time concerning the slow drip theory. Some states that are traditionally anti-African American in governmental hierarchy have the most oppressed legal systems that are designed to keep people of color incarcerated as a process because in some states incarceration is BIG BUSINESS (of which I will go into detail about later on in the book). The criminal justice system is the most lopsided scale of racism known to humankind.

There are more African American and Hispanic people of color incarcerated per capita than anywhere in the civilized world. Simply stated, African American people as a whole have the most people locked up in the federal system, state systems, and county and city jails all across the country, but we are only but a fraction of the United States population.

Incarceration is a multi-billion-dollar industry. In order

for any business to succeed there has to be product which is traded, sold, or invested in. The various city and county jails across the land have become virtual slave markets to where men of color are held hostage as the system of racism (just us) punishes through biases, uneven charges, accusations, and deceit. These slave markets used to be where the slaves were sold and traded in a public auction. In this era, we are sold and traded through the system (just us). We are then herded like livestock (anyone ever seen the movie "Roots"?) to modern-day plantations (prisons).

In the South (the Confederacy), slaves (inmates) work in the fields harvesting crops as they did in the 1800s, picking cotton, etc. The politicians have allowed some of their cohorts to invest in the phenom known as private prisons (private plantations). Politics, greed, old traditions, racism, and oppression more times than not have taken precedent over equality, making sense, rehabilitation, recovery, right solutions, and realistic answers that work.

Drip...drip...drip...

In Romans 8:21 it says, "Because the creation itself also will be delivered from bondage of corruption into the glorious liberty of the children of God." (See also Luke 11:29).

America, America, God shed His grace on thee... I believe wholeheartedly. Let me be clear in saying with conviction that America is the greatest country on planet Earth. I do feel, though, just like anything that is good, it has bad components within. Sort of like an operational machine that has operated for a period of time without any major problems or breakdowns. We eventually have to replace parts in the machine because they get old and worn out over a period of time because they are being used and worked. Ways of life and ways of doing things are what we as humankind thrive on. Our very survival on this earth is contingent on how our society is both set up and structured.

In retrospect in the example of that operational machine, the components of racial injustice have to be replaced with realism and honest answers. The components of inequality have to be replaced with equality in all things, not just some or a few. The components of old traditions, "the good ol' boys" of primarily elderly white men who cannot identify with the new societies of people that the states, counties, cities, and districts represent. The components of white, Black, and Hispanic people getting elected in their domiciles of national, state, county, and local districts strictly on the basis of their skin color. We have to change the way that we do business in America.

Let me be clear when I say this: NOTHING HAPPENS IN AMERICA UNTIL SOMETHING HAPPENS.

(Cause and effect) The way things once were where America did business as a country worked according to the beliefs and thinking of a society because in all actuality the way that a society thinks is how they live. Nowadays the thinking of the New Millennial is quite naturally foreign to old traditionalists because there isn't anything that bonds them to serve as common interest. The system working through the powers-that-be are quick to try and insert themselves in national crises by announcing the old, tired cliché in the way of solutions as prison reform, police reform, education reform, healthcare reform, but I've never once heard any of them announce racism reform. How about "Good ol' boy system reform?" Better yet, let's cut straight to the chase. How about "character reform" because before anything can truly and honestly be reformed, the intentions and reasons must be genuinely ready to adapt to modern thinking. Why? Simply because of agendas. The true purpose of those agendas are effective according to intent with the most important being the public's response to that issue or situation. In this area of folks, one will know real quick what is hot and what is not. Public opinion is one of the most powerful tools of persuasion known to man.

Here is a quick opinion that could be of public sentiment: more African Americans are Democrats and/or tend to be sympathetic to Democratic issues and agendas because number one, in Congress and in the Senate there are but a couple of African American Republicans, one in the Senate, for sure. Where is our voice represented there? Most Democrats that are state Representatives hail from metropolitan areas throughout the country that consist of predominantly African American people in their respective districts, guess what? The majority of those Congress people in those Congressional districts are Democrats. Therefore, they get voted in by the people that look like them.

I am not a political person, thus I'll be the first to say it: not all Democrats have our interest at heart either when certain issues arise concerning nationwide racial injustices. Certain African American Democrats seem to crawl out from under the rock that they've been under for years and utter the same tired speech of "meet me at the mountain top." I believe that out of nothing else but respect that we even tolerate these people simply because the movement that it was back when the same mentalities aren't involved. The traditionalist thinking pinpoints us as being brainwashed. NOT. They get in the front of us and give fiery speeches of retribution in the same speech and breath they advocate peace. This is how these career politicians have played us like a funky piano.

I remember and instance when myself, a local Houston disc jockey (DJ Wrecktified), Rapper Pyrex of Houston, and my brother for life Mike Prince of Rap-A-Lot Records were doing the anti-gang circuit all over the place. I had just published my second book entitled "Gangland...I Raised Your Kids" (Amazon.com), which is an anti-gang book. I had created TGI1, which stood for gang-initiative. The one stood for the first of its kind in Houston. No politics involved.

I had met the Honorable Robert Muhammad at the radio station because I was a guest on DJ Wrecktified's Wednesday program. I had shown up kind of early and was introduced to Mr. Muhammad who himself had a program called Connect the Dots at the same radio station. We exchanged cell phone numbers and went our separate ways. He said that he would tune in to DJ Wrecktified's show to listen to us. The next day he called me and told me how much he liked the show and he insisted that we meet soon. We ended up meeting the following Saturday at a popular restaurant on Highway 288 in the Third Ward of Houston. Bottom line, he was interested in my book, my message, and TGI1. He asked me about various venues then he proposed one. He then suggested that we do it at the oldest and largest African American church in Houston. I told him that I would get back with him. We shook hands and parted.

When I got in my car, I called Mike and told him what had just transpired. He simply said that it was my call, do what I felt was right. To make a long story short, I ended up calling Mr. Muhammad back and graciously declined. We had it at the New Beginnings Church under the leadership of Pastor Clifton Walker, Sr.

I went back on the radio show leading up to the forum, taking Pastor Walker and Pastor Steven Floyd with me (Saltmine Ministries Church) to promote the forum. See, by that large church being a prominent church in the community of Houston I knew whom it would attract. By the brothers of the Nation being decked out in their bow ties and attire I knew whom that would attract as well. I didn't want anything to take away from the main theme and true purpose of the forum, which was to help young people and their families to provide both intervention and prevention as an alternative to gang lifestyle. I didn't want to take a chance of this opportunity being somehow overshadowed or distracted by other agendas.

Am I advocating that there was malicious intent? NO WAY! What I am saying, though, is that I wasn't willing to roll the dice. This forum wasn't about me, the Nation, or anyone that was an organizer. It was about the people that needed to hear the message of what these brothers and myself had to say to them.

I learned long ago that sometimes things, both positive and negative, occur simply because life is lived, not on the premises of how it is viewed. Nothing is promised by man that can be guaranteed. At times glamour and/or fame take away from people taking a point or even a movement seriously simply because everyone's main focus isn't on why we are here but on who is here.

In 2020 we as a nation experienced a pandemic that was two-fold. COVID-19 took the world by storm and declared war on the United States of America. I feel that a big portion of our tensions as a society and attitudes were a direct result of the COVID-19 virus simply because number one, we were not prepared for anything of this magnitude as a nation, number two, the leadership of this country in the past four years had been so accustomed to conducting world affairs and national affairs as though we were on a gigantic reality TV show in which they had not a clue as to what should be done when real crisis management was needed, and number three, economics took center stage. People were literally afraid that the human race was about to parish.

This pandemic reminded me of some old movies that I watched long ago concerning how things would be if a world catastrophe happened. "The Book of Eli" with Denzel Washington and "Mad Max" with Mel Gibson came to mind.

Economics pertaining to the economy of each state is a huge deciding factor when it comes to and pertains to many important decisions that financially affect them in one way or the other. This pandemic of the coronavirus provided beyond a shadow of a doubt that reality has to present itself in order that we may witness firsthand that it isn't always fair. In saying that the absolute strength and survival of a nation and the states' economies is the mainstay of its very existence, state government showed us that human life is secondary to the survival of the state. State governments throughout the nation briefly closed their doors then reopened their cities and towns during the pandemic, which only progressed the virus even more, in turn causing a wave of increased cases in record proportions daily.

The tensions from the pandemic of people not being able to work, not being able to socially live normally, and just being in constant fear of the person standing in the grocery store line next to you…fear can be one's worst enemy or one's greatest motivating factor. If one doesn't know how to channel that fear it most definitely can be the single most illusionary events that one has ever experienced. Fear causes us to at times lose sight of the reality that is right in our faces.

I feel that because of the mandatory lockdowns that went into effect at the onslaught of the pandemic. People had a lot of time on their hands that normalcy didn't afford them before. People had time to reevaluate a lot of things concerning their lives and reflect on their situations and life circumstances. A lot of things that they normally wouldn't give a thought to because of the per se rat race called life. People had time to assess all of the things going on all around them through books, television, news feeds, and so forth.

In retrospect, some folks became frustrated, irritated, and felt caged in like an animal, thus anything that furthermore pushed those frustrations were and became immediate targets of their ire. Fear of the unknown is perhaps the greatest and most suffocating fear of them all.

COVID-19 was literally unknown to all of us as a society. The United States of America is the greatest country on earth. We as a nation were engaged by an enemy that killed regardless of race, creed, or nationality. COVID-19 landed on American soil and laid havoc to our economy, killed thousands upon thousands of people, and it exposed pantomimic leadership.

In retrospect, COVID-19's onslaught (fear) woke up and united a nation that is burned out on the old ways of thinking and doing business. Multi-racial protest signaled that not just African Americans are saying through unified voices and though unified actions, "I can't breathe." Get your knee of racial and social injustice off of all of our necks! This era of people are signaling to the police, to the governments, Congress, to the Senate, to the president, to the Supreme Court, that you must turn the water off! We are not going to accept this any longer.

The old norm isn't normal anymore, it isn't our norm.

Furthermore, our thoughts don't intertwine with our great, great, great grandparents' thinking. Simply, they thought as they thought because of who they were and where they were. Likewise, we think like we do because of both who and where we are. That means that as a collective movement and as a multi-racial unified people we have drawn a line in the sand, so to speak. We have as one decided to stand against immoral wrongs, unjustifiable wrongs, ethical wrongs.

I can't believe that any man or woman can truly claim that they are American in heart and not believe in the freedoms and rights of others. America is supposed to be the leading example of true democracy. America is characterized all over the world as the leading example of how every country's government should operate. In saying that America's success is attributed to how it is governed, which in turn reflects the true genius within a democracy, is a state of society characterized by formal equality of rights and privileges.

A question can be derived from that particular definition, one would think. Do we really live in a democracy? Is it in name only? I mean, let's be real, shall we? What word sticks out the most in that definition? Well, to me I zeroed in on one particular word—EQUALITY. Equality means the same. When everyone is afforded the same rights and privileges, that is a true democracy. Not in most things. Not even in certain things. But democracy is equality in all things.

When we as African American people are afforded the same rights as others in positive police interactions (not in the back of a police car), when we can statistically stop filling up federal and state prison systems, when we can stop being the majority in the county and city jails because of laws and rules that directly target people of color, we can then say that America is a democracy.

When we realize that the building of walls are built so that we cannot see reality. Walls divide and division is a tactic of evil. When the police stop killing folks in the name of law and order, then we can attest that we live in a democracy. When we can peacefully protest without aggressive pushback and consequences, then we can realistically proclaim that we live in a democracy.

The only two rights it seems like African Americans have in America is the right to be prosecuted while being black, and the right to be silent while the system of racial and social injustice continues to impose its will.

Drip…drip…drip…

A certain guy who was elected president of the United States got elected not by the will of the people, but by running a strategic campaign of division and chaos, sort of like the "vini, vidi, vici" statement from a conquerer that I once heard tell of, which translates to, "I came, divided, and conquered." This guy's message of division and racism is truly a first on many levels.

Division is a tool to confuse the mind and thoughts of others. When the mind is made up pertaining to a cause or an issue of controversy, then more times than not we are going to assert our right and will in the general directions that our brains and hearts lead us to. When division is inserted into that equation, we at times become hesitant and unsure. At times we even doubt facts and truths right before us. Division gives life to the questioning of one's own morals, ethics, and truths because unlike some things many things that come to divide only make sense to that part of one's brain that actually wants to believe in the chaos or the object of the division. In other words, not the person nor object that is the center of the division because they are only one person with only their own opinions and ideologies maybe pushing their agendas of division trying to divide.

We, however, have our own minds and our own opinions, which tells me that if an individual embraces hate and racial injustice as an ally, then he or she did not all of a sudden swallow the message of division and then woke up to decide that they were racist, but they have been closet racists all of this time. They only needed for someone or some cause to come along to make it even remotely okay to come out of that closet of racism, hate, and division.

In Luke 11:17 it says, "But He knowing their thoughts said to them every kingdom divided against itself is brought to desolation, and a house divided against a house falls."

Anything divided can't last. At times it may appear that is the way to go, but even the word of God says that it will fall. Being a believer, I will say that division is a device of the enemy to take away our focus on good things and positive solutions that come from God. Peace, love, joy, happiness are all of the things that come from God.

I have come to a point in this book to where I have to speak, or in this case write, about an issue that is near to my heart. That issue is the American voting system in electing the President of the United States. Too much has happened for me to not speak on this subject. I feel that part of what we are going through as a society at this moment has to do with the voting system (nationally).

This certain guy made a believer out of me that it does matter who the President of the United States is. The old standard in the African American "hoods" was it didn't matter who the president was, it didn't affect us one way or another other than support President Obama because he was Black. Out of respect of that fact "the hood" really didn't too much care. We didn't really feel an enormous overhaul or financial gain because of his presidency. However, our ambition levels and inspirational levels soared to new heights. We felt like this was our country too. Some of us took ownership for the first time in our lives in the United States of America. We felt invested.

Under the authoritarian rule of this other guy that was the president during the writing of this book, we as a country were in trouble the very moment that he conjured up in his mind to run for office. Maybe I'm the only one that has thought this or asked this question, but if the reason for a national voting system is based on the merit of the will of the people, why doesn't the popular vote count? I mean, in state, county, and city elections, the tally of the votes by the citizens determines who they want running their government. Why is there a difference on the national stage? If the reason for a voting system is for the people whom, by the way, this country is made up of, and those people go to the polls to vote, a vote is a formal expression of the choice of an individual as to whom they feel the most qualified to fill a position and/or to do a job. A person votes for someone because they have confidence and faith in that person that they will perform in a competent capacity being the voice of the voter that assisted to put them in office. If, in fact, the United States voting system is a legitimate way in which the people insert a man or woman into the highest office in the land, then why doesn't the final tally of the people's will count? Why is there a general election if the votes in general don't count?

The question is often asked why there is often minimal Black participation in presidential elections. This is one reason. We feel that our votes don't count. The common word on the street is they are going to do what they want to do no matter who we voted for.

In essence, only the Electoral College's votes count. The Electoral College is supposed to be a reflection of the people and their votes. However, that doesn't always occur. Therefore, we get what we got. Every state is allowed so many electoral votes, some more than others. This was put into play by the forefathers of this country, which means that the president doesn't have to have the confidence in all of America to become the president. He or she only has to have the confidence of the states that possess the most electoral votes.

I feel that the electoral system was adequate during the times that it was created. I think that it too is one of the systems of national government that is outdated as well. It's almost as though the Electoral College is the secret society that governs the country.

I truly believe that America is the land of opportunity without a doubt. I believe that form a financial standpoint that there are cities in America that benefit African Americans more so than others. I reside in one of those cities. Our mayor is an African American man to who I must admit is a true politician. Is that a good thing or a bad thing? Sometimes it is both—sometimes good, sometimes bad. I will say this, though, about our mayor—he's no dummy. He knows how to play "the game."

The old traditional society are often harsh judges, however. They flinch at being judged (I dare you). In today's thinking people aren't as much put into categories like they used to, meaning more than likely if a person with tattered clothing entered a restaurant, instead of someone calling the police on him someone would buy him a meal. I believe that the thinking of today's society focuses more on empathy, familiarity, enjoyment, and like-minded ventures than anything else.

Traditionalist thinking of racial and social injustice is only relevant because people try to keep this way of being alive through their stupidity. Then after the pushback that they are sure to get from the public they always issue apologies. My thing with that is why apologize for how you are? If you were a racist yesterday, you are still a racist today. Hate doesn't turn on and off like a light switch.

Just like a mind was conditioned to hate it has to be reconditioned not to hate. We have to appeal to that portion of our brain that stores what makes sense and to that portion of our brain that stores reason.

I witnessed on the news a couple of days ago the very sad incident of a Baltimore, Maryland African American women and her minor child being refused service at a restaurant in Baltimore because of the way that her minor son was supposedly dressed. The mom videorecorded the entire incident on her cell phone. While recording it was discovered that a Caucasian child about the same age as the African American child was dressed similarly. The difference, however, was that the Caucasian child was seated already and eating with his own parents.

The 2020 protests were in theory about these types of injustices. We are clearly saying don't treat us differently because you can't relate. I do understand that any business has to have rules and/or guidelines in order that they run appropriately. I get it, but do not try and enforce a rule or compliance protocol and not include everyone.

In many businesses I often do see a sign that states, "We reserve the right to refuse service." In retrospect, we the people reserve the right to expose these types of businesses that condone racial and social injustices. Make sure if service is refused that it is refused to everyone for the same things. In that way of doing things there are never questions of moral, ethical, nor biased professional standards.

In reality there were two characters being conditioned at the same time during that incident: the African American child and the Caucasian child both. From the interview that I saw the little Black kid knew perfectly well what was going on around him. He understood that all the fuss taking place at his expense hadn't anything to do with the way that he was dressed. He learned quite clearly that his Blackness has limitations. I felt sorry for the white family in that they were just out trying to get a bite to eat and were forced into a national headline by a bigot restaurant manager in that he didn't consider the "smoke" that this would cause. The little white kid learned that his whiteness is at times the currency of his entitlement.

Drip…drip…drip…

As the thinking of society changed, so did many values change as well. Historical markers such as statues and namesakes became reminders of a portion of American history that the new era of like-minded folks are ashamed of. These so-called historical markers and painful reminders were once celebrated and looked upon as icons and people of deep, rich heritages that took pride in being slave owners, murderers, segregationists, and hate-mongers. Many of these people in which statues are erected for buildings and military bases named after represented then and now shrines of a sort, and "heroism" as one U.S. President was quoted as saying.

These things represented, these people represented, what the United States of America stands for in thought, way of life, being, and they represented the very identity of the people that are in charge and govern this nation within the cities, counties, parishes, and states. These monuments, historical markers, and statues by their very presence gives hate its most visible platform, even more so in the Southern states because many of those monuments and statues that are visible are in honor of Southern white guys who died and fought to keep Black folks as slaves.

A mind can be changed, and a will can be broken, but when someone is willing to lay their life on the line and they actually die for that cause and/or belief, then that belief or cause was <u>who they were</u>. It doesn't matter how we as ancestors and modern-day thinkers would like to feel or think about our family trees on how certain ancestors did things way back when up until they were laid to rest. The facts are what they are. Great, great, great grandpa GEW was and died a bigot, racist, hate-filled mess and there isn't anything that we can do about it.

I believe that as a people when we trace down family trees and ancestry we at times discover not-too-good things about some of our ancestors back in the day. We cannot undo what has taken place. I feel that anyone who goes through their life trying to make amends will spend the rest of their lives incomplete simply because there is no such thing. No one, thing, or amount of money can make up for the cruelty and inhumane treatment the Black folk endured back then. Nothing can make up for the lives lost or the souls ruined. Nothing can make up for the feeling of being caged against your will.

Don't get me wrong, bondage and slavery of the physical kind has been outlawed long ago and makes it illegal to own another human being up to a certain degree (I will explain later on in this book). However, bondage and slavery of one's mind and of one's will remains an old and destructive manipulation tactic that has been the American norm and still exists to try and have a nonverbal say in this country.

The actions of racial and social injustice tell us that the belief in inequality is yet prevalent within the minds and hearts of those that are avid racist elitists that do their very best to push their agendas through the disguise of political, social, and economic policies and in their governmental agencies. They do this by poisoning the minds of society with racial stunts such as trying to repeal DACA, which was an act that President Obama signed into law, police brutality, and the cold-blooded murder of African American and Hispanic American people by the same folks that are supposed to protect them from that very thing.

Racist stunts such as the American justice system auctioning off people of color within the judicial courtrooms, sending them to legal plantations. I don't think that anyone, should they profess to be a realist, wonder why there are violent protests. As a matter of fact, the question of the matter should have been when, simply because if people have been marching arm in arm decade after decade in peaceful protest and peaceful demonstrations, and still in 2020 no one was listening and a whole lot really has not changed, then folks start thinking of other paths to resistance.

What did change though is the thinking of society as a whole, which in turn produces a stronger will for change, which means that the way that we go about effecting that change has to evolve as well internally, which always has to lead to a change in the way that we protest.

Is violence a solution? I feel that every war has its downfalls as it too has its advantages as well. Let me be clear, violence always begets violence. So, no, it isn't a remedy to our nation's problems. I am advocating that we do whatever it sensibly takes. We have to get someone's attention, mainly the folks that run this place. Whatever it takes to let the "old guard" know that enough is enough. That the old, traditional ways of doing business in America don't work anymore in this millennial, and if they want to stay in office, if they still want say-so in the running of this country, our states, our counties, our cities, our parishes, and our towns, they too must evolve or very simply need to get out of the way so that new, fresh energy can be brought in to govern and lead a nation of different people with different beliefs, with different ideas, and most importantly, it doesn't matter the color of their skin.

The American norm is that a lot of these leaders stay in these offices and positions of governance until they die off. By that time they are so old that they are really out of touch with the people that they govern and represent. Therefore, bills get passed and legislation gets signed to accommodate their peers' interests. How can someone sign a bill against healthcare that never even visited a government-assisted hospital facility that does accept Medicare and Medicaid? Or a clinic where there are 100 percent poverty-assisted patients there waiting to be seen by a physician?

If we want real change in this country new millennials have to run for these seats and offices. If we want to flip this country's old, tired, worn-out ways of doing things and doing business, we have to stop being complacent with stimulus checks, income tax returns, HUD low income housing vouchers, and SNAP food stamp benefits. We have to look at this stuff for what they really are. These so-called benefits have been pacifiers to keep us quiet and content with having to do as little as possible for free as we prioritize the wrong things (hair, nails, the club, jewelry, clothing, etc.).

I believe that this is a movement era as it was in the '60s. The difference between then and now is that multi-racial resistance to biased actions and to social injustices is the new norm now. A unified front has been created from every walk of life, from every color of people. Unified voices are speaking loudly and let me be clear, they are getting louder and louder as the days pass. We must move in unison, not against the law, but to change them and make them fair, equal, and apply to everyone so that they will fit within the society that they govern. Society should not have to conform to a couple to a few hundred people that legislate with their personal thoughts, will, thinking, and reasoning of the people in which they govern simply because true governance and leadership is about the people in which they serve, not about the society in which they govern.

Anyone can give orders and set rules on what to do and when to do it. Real governance is when a body of individuals can come up with positive growth as a solution instead of worrying about growing their own bank accounts. True governance evolves according to the era that they are governing in. I can think of a group of ladies in Washington DC right now that have a few of the old guard kind of shook up because they are new millennial thinkers with fresh, new energy giving the old, tired establishment pause, doubt, and I have to say it because it is the truth…fear.

I am an advocate in a leader has to feel the pain of their

people that are crying out to them and depending on them to get the job done, point blank period. I always ask the question, how can someone help another if they cannot see the object of their despair? True governance isn't about infrastructural fighting amongst parties that disagree, not because a piece of legislation suggested won't work for the people, but the parties agree or disagree not because it was a bad bill or a good bill, but the decision about and concerning folks' lives is made on the premises of whom suggested it.

Come on, people. It isn't about who introduces a law or a bill or a legislative agenda.

Society tends to mold itself at times through the actions or inactions of the people that govern a particular country and government which they do set the standards to how a society should live and conduct their overall business while operating within the confounds of the governmental model of freedom (the United States) and democracy. As a government behaves, so do the people follow suit. Perfect example: If there is a chaotic administration in the White House there is going to be in turn a chaotic Congress and an even more chaotic Senate, thereby creating a chaotic country of people. Let me be clear on what I am about to say—there isn't anything good that can be produced from anything bad.

When two jackals mate they produce another jackal. The responsibility of whom is in certain positions in this country, states, counties, parishes, is entirely on the American people. What is really weird I suppose is at times we are consciously aware of the imminent dangers that some of these people present to our peace, harmony, and our overall making-sense thinking, but that part of our humanistic selves more times than not want to believe in the overall good of others as we seek hope, as we seek change, as we seek for a voice that speaks for what is right and just for the people that still hold on to the faith in one another. Therefore, we take all of these things with us to the polls and voting stations based on not so much as what we've seen or heard both from and about a candidate, but we take all that we hope for to the polls and voting stations.

Simple question: How can I vote for a human being that I don't even know? We can only hope that they will do the right and decent things when in office. Voting in public officials is like going to a casino and dropping a coin into a slot machine. Every now and then you'll win something for sure, but one thing is for certain if nothing else, you'll never have the chance to win if you don't play.

When voting for public officials, if you vote there is always the chance that the person that you voted for may prevail. I always say these two things to people about voting: 1) If you are unhappy with the way things are go vote and encourage others to vote as well; and 2) If you didn't go vote please don't whine about the results.

I believe that in state and local elections that we the people put who we vote for in office, as also we vote in our congressmen and senators as well. Under the present system I feel that the present system gives us (Electoral College) a voice but not the final say in who gets elected to the presidency. I do believe that it does involve politics and another book to be written for sure. Stay tuned.

What really is irritating about politics I suppose more than anything is when a member of Congress or Senate sides with an injustice of an administration. Also, when a politician comes out and tries to play on the American public's intelligence by telling us that we didn't see something that we did see and didn't hear something that we clearly heard. Again, these are the traditional games of illusion that are played to confuse the thoughts of the people, sort of like a magician's sleight of hand trick, only instead of cards these people play with our very lives, livelihoods, and with our very existence as a society.

In 2020 we saw major corporations change their brands and deep Southern states such as Mississippi make adjustments to their racist state flag that hung high and proud at its state Capitol for decades. I believe that the rebranding of certain products are two-fold, meaning the syrup company had their particular brand for quite some time, and as we know the face of that brand did not own that particular brand, nor did she have shares or stock invested in that company. Furthermore, she did not sit in any era on the board of directors of said company that was synonymous with merely her picture. I'm willing to bet a nickel to a dollar that she didn't even work for that particular brand. So, how does one come up with the branding, or in this case, the face of a certain brand?

The crazy thing about that is Black folks have been buying and using this product for decades without complaint. I am guilty. If no one noticed as the years changed, so did the woman's appearance on the bottle change as well. See, the lady's likeness never changed because trust me we knew who she was, no introductions needed, but her appearance always seemed to blend in with the era. She always had her name, maybe sixth generation, but she was still who she was created to be to America, which was the overall branding of the company in general, concerning both the image and the namesake, which was clearly indicating a Black female servant, possibly indicating (on the original bottle) a Black woman in slavery.

Many things go unnoticed within our society because our main focus is primarily on what is popular to like or dislike. In today's world of new millennial thinkers it seems that the world is under the microscope. Everything that is done is seen. Everything that is said is heard. A body doesn't have to tell you where they are for you to pinpoint their exact location. In saying that this is a very different world that we live in, of course the millennial folks are going to view many things quite differently simply because they are not looking at the world through the same glasses and eyes as maybe the ones that need new glasses or corrective eye surgery so that they may see better.

I believe that said syrup company didn't just change their minds about the brand because someone just woke up one morning and decided that the person on their bottle represented one of the oldest racial profiles and insensitive stereotypes ever. They didn't care because that brand made money. I believe that nothing was ever said because in the past eras and times in the past the old slave mentality was, "Why stir up something if we didn't have to?" and we were complacent and passive because we were conditioned by our ancestors and great-grandparents to not make the good white folks mad at us.

Remember that I said earlier on that things that come from the inside of us cannot be turned on and off like a light switch. Only things that we are conditioned to do can be changed gradually. Ways of thinking and ways of doing things must change in order for us to move constructively forward as a nation of people (Americans).

In 1861 seven Southern states set up the Southern States of America. On February the 8th, 1861 Jefferson Davis was named the president of those Southern states appropriately named The Confederacy. On April 12th of that same year the Confederates fired on Fort Sumter in Charleston, South Carolina. They captured the Fort two days later. On April the 15th, one day after the capture of Fort Sumter, the then-President of the United States Abraham Lincoln, called up 75,000 volunteers to fight against the Confederacy. On April the 19th President Lincoln ordered the blockade of all of the southern ports, cutting off vital exports to the Confederate soldiers. By May 11th other states had seceded or withdrawn from the Union.

In May 1862 one of the most significant battles of the Civil War took place. The Union took New Orleans, LA as well as Gettysburg, PA in 1863, which also signaled a turning point. 1865 saw Robert E. Lee surrender 27,800 Confederate soldiers to General Ulysses Grant in Virginia. Likewise did J.E. Johnston surrender over 31,000 to General Sherman in North Carolina.

President Lincoln was assassinated in April of that same year. On December 6th, 1865 the 13th Amendment to the Constitution of the United States of America was enacted abolishing slavery (proposed by Congress January 31, 1865 and ratified December 6, 1865).

Section 1: Neither slavery nor involuntary servitude except as punishment for crime whereof the party shall have been duly convicted shall exist within the United States or any other place subject to their jurisdiction.

Section 2: Congress shall have power to enforce this Article by appropriate legislation.

See, nothing had really changed. The Constitution abolished slavery but really didn't abolish slavery completely. This, my dear reader, is where the exact root of the problem of racial and society injustice lies.

I've been preaching this message for a long time: Incarceration is legal slavery! Someone got creative and figured out how to continue to make money off of it. The federal and state prisons (plantations) are holding pens (like livesock) and sweat shops. The Constitution of the United States does give other human beings, as in the government, legal rights to hold another human being in slavery if they are convicted of a crime. Therefore, in all actuality slavery was never completely abolished. Freedom came with provisions and slavery remained.

So, in truth 400 years in captivity and slavery right now today it is yet legal to own slaves in the United States of America. We can buy our freedom back with doing whatever time as a sentence that is imposed on us. The judge may as well say, "I sentence you to life on the plantation."

Isolated incidents always make people notice what is immediately going on all around them, for the truthful fact is police don't murder people everyday (one day is too much), therefore, it isn't normal. So, when it does happen, we all pay attention to it, which in turns gives fuel to the question why does it ever happen at all? No, it doesn't happen everyday that a police officer kills and murders an unarmed citizen. The fuss is about that it should not happen at all.

Drip…drip…drip…

The mindset is harder to change in mentalities of old because maybe those mentalities were conditioned by success, and with certain successes comes wealth. With most wealth power isn't far behind. These three things, I believe, may be humankind's greatest motivating factors. Likewise, I believe that they are also humankind's greatest of downfalls as well. I believe that in the quest for success, wealth, and power, more times than not during that climb it's inevitable that we may have to step on the heads of some people so that we may ascend to the top. Most of the time it doesn't matter how hard that we try, someone is going to get their feelings hurt. "Stepped on heads," as the saying goes, "may not ever be intentional, but yes, it is sure to happen.

What is wrong with type of thinking is that we disrespect the rights of others so that we can remain powerful, wealthy, and successful.

I've often heard that the key to trying to please everybody is the key to failure. I believe that the key to success is wise choices. Often what got us to a certain point that won't sustain us means we must evolve in our thinking simply because the path to a certain point isn't the measuring stick simply because true success is now, pass successes are history, a check already cashed and spent.

I am an avid believer in to keep one's mind enslaved is far worse than being in any form of physical oppression for two reasons. A body can escape physical oppression by simply removing themselves from the equation. We can drive, we can walk, or we can run away, etc. The mind is the starting place of all thought, which in turn leads to all actions because our mind has to send signals to our body to move. The mind controls our will, therefore, when the mind is enslaved so is the will. When our will is enslaved we at times become voluntarily enslaved to accept whatever will be, will be.

This is what the old traditionalists of this country have been employing as a tactic for decades. The terminology I believe that we use is, "They knock the fight out of you." I call this destructive manipulation. Once they freed people conditionally in a physical sense, they figured out how to enslave them in other ways mentally.

I've come to learn that when a human being's will is enslaved they cease to exist as their own person. They become broken and useless to themselves or anyone around them. Additionally, when they are broken, they become a byproduct at times of that in which broke them, almost like a pawn or puppet in which they just accept whatever it is that they must. They become passive to injustice. They become indifferent to inequality of any kind. They become accepting of the idea that they are inferior. When the will is broken we become afraid of reality.

A family member once told me, "Now, don't go ruffling feathers, making those people mad at you." This statement wasn't surprising considering where this family member grew up in the South. Their mentality was to not create "smoke," just live a life that God has allowed me to live and mind my own business. I love this family member dearly but even they must come to know that racial injustice and social injustice is not only my business, but it is all of our business!

The police brutality, the senseless murders by police, the political machine of immoral politics, the praising and honoring of pro-slavery figures with statues and monuments, and in the mental and social racist enslavement of thought by "trying to knock the fight out of me" mentally--it is my business as well as it is everyone's business that believes that there is one God of everyone who does not differentiate from African American to Caucasian to Asian to Hispanic American. God has given all of humankind the sense of what is right and what is wrong, so even those that may be born blind have a situated within knowledge of God, for Romans 1:19-20 says, "Because of what may be known of God is manifest in them, for God has shown it to them." Not only are divine attributes clearly seen in humankind, but they be seen all around us as well in the way of nature and all things.

The ways that we do business in this country is in fact changing. As I've stated numerous times before, division is a tactic and ploy that people with evil intent employ to confuse the mind. An example of that is a certain president retweeted a video showing a white man yelling and screaming, "White power!" Jeez…this guy. Dude, if you haven't noticed, I mean, after all you are only the president, racial tension is at an all-time high. This is what this guy does. He creates division through controversy. He diverts attention from one issue to another. I've heard that there is some more "smoke" going on that he and his people don't want to draw attention to, which of course involves the Russians, Putin, and company paying Taliban insurgents bounties to assassinate American soldiers in Afghanistan. From my understanding, that president and Putin are buddies, so quite naturally his political party is looking at him asking, "What the heck?"

The American military represents America. They protect and they serve our nation. So, here we have the Commander In Chief's buddy allegedly murdering these men and women that keep us safe from people like Putin. "Humpty Dumpty (president) sat on a wall (immigration), Humpty Dumpty had a great fall (Congressional impeachment), and all the king's horses and all the king's men (his political party) couldn't put Humpty together again."

Black Lives Matter is a movement like no other before it. It has touched a nation of people and brought awareness to the world. Most people that don't, won't, can't, and/or refuse to understand what this movement is about point fingers and declare that the movement in itself is in fact first a racist slogan and movement as it speaks volumes to imply that only black lives matter and no else's lives matter. PA...LEASE! Stop it. I get it. In a country where the history and norm of a society is based on power, control, and wealth, this has been the means and the standard of a people that have so desired to rule and establish themselves on the level of kings, monarchs, and aristocrats, believing that the color of one's skin entitled them to be as so simply because of bloodlines passed down from aristocrat to aristocrat, slave owner to slave owner, racist to racist. By look, by sound, and by feel the scale of equality has been tipped for a long time. It is very often shown that as a singular race of people that Black lives are expendable. The falsehood derives from the old lifestyles of Black people being property only, therefore replaceable. After all, Black folk weren't in public office, which meant that they had no say so in the running of the country. They didn't own any businesses that brought jobs into the cities and towns across the nation, nor were they the consumers that fed the American economy through purchasing power.

In the old expendable theory African American people did not command a presence because all property can be replaced. Our presence was felt, however, at a time when white supremacy had the world as an audience. In 1936 during the Olympic games when Jessie Owens destroyed the track and field records and won four gold medals for the United States, this was significant for several reasons, with the main one extinguishing the theory by Germany's then-leader (Adolph Hitler) that white people were dominant, thus the superior race in all things by way of bloodline. Joe Louis won the boxing heavyweight championship the following year.

These historical feats did not, however, make us equal as human beings according to popular belief. It did give fuel to others on how they could profit off of Mr. Owens' and Mr. Louis' history-making moments. The sad thing about both of these men of history is that although they were history in themselves, they yet had to drink out of separate water fountains as did white folks. They yet had to enter a restaurant through the back door. And if they so chose public transportation they yet had to ride at the back of the bus.

I believe as time changed so did the thinking of those in charge. The evolution (change) of a society does exist, meaning nothing stays the same. In order for a society to grow and progress our thought process has to grow and progress as well. I truly believe that those in charge were not ready to balance the scales of equality because that would have required them to maybe give up some power and control, which meant that they would maybe have to share in some wealth as well.

Therefore, the system spoon fed us a little bit at a time. This is how they have always kept us under control passively. Thurgood Marshall was named as Supreme Court Justice in 1967, the very first African American to be so named. We as a race of people saw that appointment as a major stepping stone. However, he was only one vote and one opinion on the court, yet and still in a system of injustice and inequality.

I have learned that sports are an expression of African American people through the mere physicality of being Godly gifted and talented to run faster, jump higher, and dominate athletically like no other race of people on planet Earth. Personally, athletic contests of various sorts emotionally lift us. To witness our favorite team or favorite athlete compete with and against one another is a thing of beauty to say the least. Let's face it, everyone loves a winner! The NFL and the NBA became worldwide must-see TV. Baseball was American's game, but the NFL and the NBA monopolized entertainment and put the genre of sports in a proverbial "choke hold." These sports took on a face of their own, therefore the participants did too, which made us not expendable any longer.

In these times athletes, entertainers, rappers, etc. aren't really looked at as role models as they used to be back in the day because the new millennial really see role model admiration as "lame" (not hip). Role models used to be people that we aspired to be like because of their success and very different lifestyles. That isn't the case any longer for several reasons, one of them being social media brings these people to our lives up close and personal 24 hours a day, seven days a week if we so choose. In our living rooms, driving in our cars, at our doctor's office, we have immediate access to these celebrities whenever we like, making them not so much as role models but almost as peers. Sort of like a neighbor that we admire for being famous. These people become our friends because we are exposed to every facet of their lives through social media. Almost like family, a bond is created sort of because we get to witness and gain so much knowledge about that individual through YouTube, Instagram, Facebook, Twitter, Snapchat, and many more. The point is that establishing personal relationships with professional athletes, celebrities, and movie stars is the normal now. Thus, they become people that we can share joy, pain, experiences, situations, issues, events, and lifestyles with.

In Black Lives Matter we share all of these things through life-altering struggles that keep plaguing this country in racial and social injustices because African American people are statistically the most incarcerated, the most murdered, the most oppressed, race of people in the United States of America. So, it looks like on the surface that Black lives don't matter. That we are yet and still expendable every time an African American person is murdered by police. We are not expendable. Black lives matter. In sentencing laws and bills such as the Crime Bill of 1994 which locked up more African Americans than any legislation ever, black lives matter. Each time a sentence of incarceration is imposed in the system of "just us" that is more times than not in excess compared to our Caucasian counterparts, we are not expendable. Black lives matter. When statues, monuments, and historical markers remain erected honoring symbols of hate and racism, our integrity, respect, and dignity is not expendable. Black lives matter. Black lives matter simply because the God of white lives, brown lives, yellow lives, created Black lives as well as he created all lives.

Just to reemphasize on my point of a bunch of old people trying to run a country full of new millennial thinkers that have totally different ideas and ways of living life, I was watching a TV show not too long ago and one of the politician's wives came on the show and was talking about the COVID-19 pandemic. First off, I really respect this lady on the merit that she is as mentally and intellectually sharp as a tack. She spoke about the country getting back on track, electing her husband, and why he is the perfect candidate. She was on a roll. I was "turned up" as possibly can be. I am sure that everyone viewing the show was ready to head to the polls right then and there to go vote. Then she said, "Kids need to be able to go outside to play kick the can." What??? Okay, what kids are these? Whose kids in this millennium plays kick the can? Is kick the can out on PlayStation? Is kick the can played as a video game? Can it be played as virtual reality? Is it downloadable? Is it an app?

I am by no means knocking her message. Leadership change is definitely needed ASAP within this country. I get the primary theme, however, when we are trying to both convince people of our capabilities to lead and co-lead our lives are always under the microscope and the enemy is always looking for an advantage. We have to do our due diligence in all things so that we just don't sound like the normal swamp dwellers but we grow with true change, we radiate honesty and sincerity, and we promise things and a brand-new way of doing things with conviction. What is crucial to any message is the willingness of a man or woman to speak and represent a country's ideas, economics, dreams, hopes, fundamentals, equalities, and fairness of a nation of modern thinking people that really believe in true change for all.

In this thinking, Black lives do matter simply because down through the history all the way to now they never have. So, in unison with perhaps millions of voices we are shouting from the rooftops, from the courtrooms, from the various federal and state prisons, from up under the knees of police officers around the nation, I CAN'T BREATHE. Get your knees up off of our necks, from the murders throughout various counties in the South of African Americans in police custody, from all racial and social injustices of African American people. We are saying as one nation under God that Black lives matter.

See, this movement isn't about the race of the subject entirely. Black Lives Matter isn't just being championed by people of color (therefore, it doesn't qualify as a hate movement). When we witness rallies, we see on television and in every news outlet possible people of all races, creeds, and colors wearing caps, shirts, holding signs supporting this movement, these are Americans of free will, free thinking, that are all in full agreement concerning the equalities and God-given freedoms of other human beings no matter the color of their skin.

    I truly believe that alternative teaching has to take place in the way of diversity forums, classes, seminars, and curriculums simply because, as I've stated before, some people just have to be reprogrammed and reconditioned. Others have to learn to coexist with folks that look different than them, come from different cultural, racial, educational, family, religious, and economic backgrounds. The most beautiful thing about diversity training that I've lectured at or taught is that people learn about other folks because they really want to.

    Yes, we are all different in many ways, but we are all alike in many ways as well. We have different opinions, different ideas, different likes, dislikes. I am convinced this is so because God created us all with different characters and characteristics, thus we all have our own ways in which we travel mentally, emotionally, and spiritually in order that we may get to a certain point concerning our way of processing things. Most of the time the journey does have an impact on us once we reach our destination of what's left remaining of what we haven't used up to get there (time, energy, relations, money, careers, etc.). The actual journey does form the basis of part of what we believe simply because in that journey through life we gained a boatload of experience along the way. When we learn things about others, we in turn learn a lot about ourselves. In diversity learning these things become obvious simply because in order to learn something about something or someone other than what we are accustomed to as a way of life we must understand that we all have a central fundamental purpose for being here in the first place.

    If I could sit every race of folk down at one table then prick the finger of everyone present so that a smidge of blood would show, I would dare anyone present to prove me wrong that everyone present has the same red blood coming from their finger, also proving that we all belong to one race of people, the human race. Further evidence that our civic differences are created by man-made situations and dark intent. We, however, don't have to remain there if we don't choose to.

The political agenda of all of our problems of racial and social injustice is, according to a couple of politicians and police experts in numerous places around the country, in the banning of chokeholds by police nationwide. I believe that this move by these officials is only putting a Band-Aid over a serious wound. Some say that it is a start to a serious overhaul of the nation's various draconian police policies and procedures. Others say that it is an obvious façade simply because the American public want any solution that is both active and progressive. We as a nation can place bans on all that we choose to. The ban of maneuvers and the ban on certain physical restraint isn't the answer.

Point is, lynchings are illegal. Have they totally stopped? No. This horrific act is banned but it has not stopped. Murder is a crime. It is illegal no matter who commits it. Has it stopped? No. Point being, when intentions are evil by anyone, being illegal and banned is only for the sake of conversation. When intent is evil, bad, evil, corrupt things happen.

Character reform is necessary. Diversity training is essential. I don't believe that Dr. EXG can teach diversity training from a platform of realism. I do believe, however, that he or she can teach from a psychological and intellectual platform that they can excel from. I believe if they have lived from experience their field of study then they are the experts to me. They know what it is that they know because they know. And believe me, as you listen you will know that they know. Teaching from both knowledge and experience is always a good recipe for a wealth of learning for everyone involved. Teaching from experience always makes the adventure personal. "I can't breathe," is personal and has become personal for a lot of people.

If an Asian person teaches diversity from an Asian American's perspective, then I can learn something from them. How? Simply because I've never been Asian American before. I cannot ever be Asian American. Thus, I don't know what the world looks like through the eyes of Asian Americans. Reality says that every race, creed, and color come from various cultures in which they were raised and so forth, producing the proverbial belief system, which in turn makes us all a diverse society in the first place. OTJ (on-the-job training) is absolute. It makes us all experts.

Part 2

MAKING SENSE

I wholeheartedly believe that new millennial folks don't have separatist inclinations simply because the educational systems are predominantly nonsegregated. Therefore, they are allowed to participate in the same events, competition, and entertainment that captures all of their attention equally, which puts them all on the same level in what they enjoy doing. No one is thinking about skin color nor race in these arenas of competition and enjoyment. It is safe to say that on the merit of whatever it is that they may be competing in and/or socializing in their enjoyment is the focus and goal. Nothing else matters.

I am thereby convinced that BIG BUSINESS has molded and

created society into like-minded individuals as well. Amazon, Nike, Jordan, PlayStation, Apple, Google, and Facebook have transformed and made their own culture of people. These businesses have in reality contributed substantially to the new society of today's thinking and attitudes of new millennial life in today's world. This applies to all people with all different skin colors, languages, and ethnic backgrounds. They together have produced the same like-minded people through their brands without prejudice.

See, back in time segregation was the invisible line that kept everyone on either side of division. In this era of now segregation and right to vote are no longer the line, which means that it is very difficult to maintain a fundamental line or common interest in the majority of folks to push hate and evil intent as normal causes. Even when "smoke" is manufactured to try and push racial division, new millennial people protest as one because they live their lives as one. I believe that in this era that no one can possibly sit idly by on the sidelines as though they are watching an updated version of reality TV. I believe that anyone that believes in God and all that we stand for as His creation and in the basic truths of what we believe in, we cannot view these travesties of racial and social injustices and not feel disrespected to the core of our being.

In seeing, hearing, and reading about a lot of this craziness through both mainstream and social media that America has come to a conclusion collectively, America is saying very clearly that this is not the country of old traditional thinkers. Those folks have built a country on dreams, hopes, and genius. They have given birth to an empire.

In retrospect, there is no such thing as a fountain of youth. People get old, traditions get even older, and technology advances, which means that it is new. It makes sense that the people that are going to be around to yet invent other stuff should be the folks that are in charge. Some people do not want to concede because selfishness is their evil intent. They continue to destructively manipulate through certain channels in certain ways, thereby producing certain results. Number one, those results are no longer acceptable in this era of thinkers and ways of life, which means that by the results being unacceptable, so are the philosophy, thinking, and the way that they arrived to those results as well.

The channels of just us, of the good ol' boy system, of unbalanced government, of outdated thinking, the channels of prehistoric lifestyle, and the channels of elitist attitudes and separatist hypothesis, which always leads to racist propaganda, are unacceptable to this new millennial of folk. Tolerance isn't the norm in this era, but action is. Furthermore, I believe that any and every solution has to fit the crises that it is formulated to manage. Example: The normal to putting out fires is with water. However, depending on what type of fire it is, water would only complicate the matter instead of helping.

This also applies to humankind problem-solving as well. There are traditionally certain modules to humanistic problem-solving based on how the human brain is supposed to function. This is also based on clinical and psychological studies and research and so forth. The system of remedy, solution, treatment, management, and cure are what form the basic modules of our medical and psychiatric norms for decades on top of decades.

We failed in 2020 during the COVID-19 pandemic because of the old ways of doing business. Let me be clear when I say that we need brand new, unique solutions for brand new, unique problems in the restoration of the economy in America. Reopening too fast only made more people more sick and the coronavirus of dire casualties only increased. The same old traditional fixes are not going to work simply because the economy has to rebound both in and from a crisis that we've never experienced before.

Most fixes derive from experiences and probabilities of happening based on research and logistics. No one has ever experienced anything of this magnitude to have made war on American soil as has this pandemic. Therefore, we as a people of the United States of America were not prepared because of the old, worn-out crisis management policies, and the old ways of government intervention policies were not prepared as we the people trusted them to be.

I am a realist therefore, I can't remain irritated at the government for not being prepared. At times we have to mentally build a bridge and get over certain things. I preach this message quite often: We cannot change history, we can however if we choose make our own or be involved with the making of today's and tomorrow's history. Remember that yesterday is a check already cashed and spent.

My irritation came about, number one, to the reactions and responses to the pandemic from the folks in charge. Two, now that it has invaded America, what's next? It is customary to look to the folks in charge when there is a crisis because that is one of the reasons that they are in charge in the first place. We as a society look to the ones in charge for viable solutions and answers. A leadership is a formidable leadership and is legitimate (not only in name) when they can provide answers and solutions to the ones that they lead.

True leadership does not care about elections in the middle

of pandemonium. They care about the condition of their people. They care about solutions to unrest, thus concerned and committed to the healing of a nation. True leadership doesn't cater to negativity, which in turn creates chaos and division. This past leadership created elitist ideologies of segregationist and separatist of the past America. The people of now, the America Now movement, whether anyone wants to embrace it now or later is the movement of the new millennial.

The American people of every race, every gender, every background, every color, from every neighborhood, every city, every state, every town, every parish, and from every religion see America Now does look like us, think like us, love like us, are one unified movement of people. America Now is us.

I am convinced that everyone should want to be a part of the solution. There were these dogs in my neighborhood that used to go from home to home knocking over trashcans on trash day, eating out of them, and spreading trash all over the streets. No one in my neighborhood would pick up the excess trash, so I took it upon myself to not only pick up the trash, but after the trash truck would come, I would wash down the street as well with a water hose that had an extension attached to it to make a long story short, one of my neighbors had an issue and had a little problem with me making the street too wet with water. My homeowner president was an ex-NBA ball player. I talked to him and he said that wasn't an issue and thanked me for trying to keep the street clean. It was a gated community and only 35 homes were in the community. I felt the trash was out of place on the street.

When we aren't part of the solution, we become sometimes directly and indirectly part of the problem. See, by not saying anything at times we become the loudest voices in the room.

Silence is oftentimes indicative of support. Silence often says I approve this message. The neighbors that didn't say anything supported my actions indirectly simply because they said nothing, giving me permission to serve my neighborhood. This is why as a people we must, with unified thinking leading to unified actions, give life to positivity and growth as the front runners in building our neighborhoods and other places where we work that things will definitely take form because when hungry for peace, solutions, unity, equality, and fairness, we have to say something. Because in reality, as we say in the hood, "a closed mouth don't get fed." This is why, or one of the reasons why, the movement is so powerful and riveting. No one is being quiet nor silent anymore. That faucet must be turned off. Orthodox racism, closet racism, racial and social injustices, not only need to be just brought to the forefront, but these things need to be addressed as well and dealt with.

I really think that racism, no matter the color of the hate, is bordering on mental illness because to hate one that you don't know personally because they are black, white, brown, or yellow tells a thinking person that someone needs professional help in dealing with some unresolved issues. Deep, dark things that only mental health professionals can assist with.

I believe that it is okay to run a test and gather evidence of something that is vile. Most of the time this is how cures and remedies are discovered. Hate is no different. In the real scope of things, we must at times love the hate away. The Bible says in John 13:25, "By this all will know that you are my disciples (followers of Christ) if you have love for one another." Unbeliever, recognize Jesus' disciples not by doctrinal distinctions nor by dramatic miracles, not by love for the lost. Disciples are recognized by their deeds of love for one another.

The Bible also says in Micah 2:1, "Woe to those who devise inequity and work out evil on their beds. At morning light they practice it because it is in the power of their hand." This is a direct warning from God to those that misuse their status to perpetrate oppression and evil intent. When we hate it is evil, therefore, against what God commands of us. Believers must love all humankind because love is the very principle of the one that it represents, which is the God of everyone and everything.

I hear people keep talking about them being frustrated because of the normal routine of life had been thrown off kilter somewhat, to others quite drastically. I don't believe that anyone is singularly bigger than the coronavirus, meaning if I by myself was stranded on an isolated island by myself I wouldn't be worried about the coronavirus. It just happens that the invasion of our nation by COVID-19, aka the coronavirus, is an equal opportunity virus. So, just in case no one has noticed, it has thrown all of our worlds into bedlam, chaos, and mayhem! This virus has turned our country upside down. No one is living in normalcy. Frustrations of all sorts are running on overtime for the entire country. This is why I stated earlier on what I said about tolerance isn't an option. Action is what folks want and are taking.

I believe wholeheartedly that we must institute the "stair step effect" into the way that we think when it pertains to advancing constructive agendas. See, comfort zones are no longer comfortable. Security blankets no longer suffice as security. So, in order to maintain what we do have and move forward we have to venture outside of those comfort zones and places that we normally feel secure in both mentally and physically. In effective problem solving we have to per se step out on our beliefs. The word of God says that faith without action is useless (void).

The stair step effect: Progressive thinking is the conscious act of using one's mind and thought process step by step. Stairways start with one step at the bottom. They usually lead upwards in a series of other stairs within a building or structure, usually stopping on each floor so that one can access each individual floor of a structure and/or building, then continuing to the next floor. We begin our lives on the bottom floor of life simply because the average person begins his or her life not the top, not even at the middle. But most hardworking folks begin their life's journey at the bottom. We call it the first floor of our lives in how we think and why we think the way that we do.

The first floor is where we are more than likely introduced to things that our parents, relatives, and loved ones introduce us to in the ways of ideologies and what they tell us about what is right and what is wrong and rules of conduct according to the closest folks to us at the time. On this floor of our life we get our first lessons in what we should believe in from a moral and ethical standards and religious point of view. The first floor of our life is our introduction to the world. Thus, our belief system is pointed in the direction most of the time where our folks want them to go.

When we start to climb and ascend on up those stairs to the second floor we've already gone through school about this time. So, as we open the door to the second floor, we walk right into our character being molded. Puberty and adolescence are behind us now. Quite naturally about this time in life we know everything (so we think). Also on this level on the second floor of our lives we oftentimes become unsure about some things simply because on the first level our parents and our loved ones protected us from potential threats to our success. On the second floor we form bonds, friendships, relationships, and allies that at times remain as so for the rest of our lives. (Level 2 in this effect is a very important and essential floor within the structure.)

The third floor represents values because as we do ascend the stairs and enter the third level door we recognize that on this level certain things start to become more important than others. Enjoyment, relationships, career, material things, everything has to be put in an order of importance on this level. This floor of life is possibly the easiest floor to remain on forever and a day simply because this is perhaps the floor to where we are the most comfortable on. We may on this floor begin to carve out our future, job, mate of our dreams, etc. Some of us may actually shut the stairwell door and never open it again once we discover all there is on this floor of life.

If we dare to climb those stairs again and progress to the next level, I am convinced that those are the folks that separate themselves from everyone else in accomplishments and success because there is that something on the inside of us (I call it a switch). I can't say, but there is a switch that is activated on the inside of us. I believe that it comes from that inner drive, ambition, determination, and will to succeed beyond the average and norm. These people are just mentally and emotionally wired differently. Some people are both happy and content with the third floor of their lives. There isn't anything wrong with that. The goals are always happiness and self-fulfillment.

I had to learn myself that everyone can't be chiefs, somebody has to fight the battle. If a certain level of success fits you and serves the purpose that you need, then embrace your happiness because only you have to live with it.

Once we enter that fourth floor however, we separate ourselves. These are the inventors, innovators, entrepreneurs, world, community, national, state, and city leaders. These are the people that are involved in life-altering movements that are impacting the world.

I have discovered that it is very easy to sit on a couch at home and give advice, feedback, and ideas to a TV that can't listen. America now is speaking to the nation and giving freedoms of all humankind a platform like never before so everyone can be heard if they choose to be. Just like opening that stairwell door and climbing to the fourth floor of our thinking and lives, we have to turn on that switch somehow.

I once wrote in one of my books that, "God never leaves us…unless we insist." The most wonderful thing about life is we can control it. We live in a time that more times than not our lifestyle dictates what happens to us in most cases. Perfect example: If a body doesn't want to die in an airplane crash, then they might ought to not get in an airplane. If I don't want to die in a car crash, I shouldn't get in a car. If I don't want to be racially profiled, then I need to change the color of my skin. I believe that is the only part of my life that I cannot control. Houstin, TX mayor said it best I believe, "I was African American before I was the mayor and I'll be African American after I am mayor."

I am convinced that the old past America and the old traditionalist ways of doing things still yet after all of these years don't get it. We are yet, and still going to be, African American, and our skin color isn't going to change. I don't believe that the intelligence, dignity, successes, entertainment, loyalty, economics, and the way that we love is what bothers them to where they hate us so. I am convinced that it is the very color of our skin that is the object of their hate. Why?

Let me be clear, when I say that the color of our skin is like a mental photo album that they go back and view and look through to remind themselves on a time when we were viewed as inferior and did as we were told without argument or pushback (power and control). I am further convinced that the most critical hate comes from those who cannot change the color of the skin no matter how powerful, wealthy, etc. Therefore, there is in fact a limitation on the scope of their power. This is what they really hate us for. We are constant reminders of their limitations.

I believe that violence in our neighborhoods in the inner cities are direct and indirect results of many things. One of them is of our own making in the creation of certain cultures. The gang culture is a popular culture in this day and age. Really it has been for a long time. This culture has too evolved as well, mainly because of the mindset of those involved. I have the opportunity to be up close and personal with these people, both male and female alike. The landscape of this culture has drastically changed. The violence was attributed in the communities to the gangs and drug dealers and once were thought to be all the same perpetrators. Not anymore. This era of community gangs doesn't imitate what once was the "gangbanger" stereotype. That too has evolved. This era sees the value of money and its own power to change lives, point blank period.

The most craziest thing that I have personally discovered about this culture is that the "hustle" is the high. The journey to the object is what they gain "street reps" on, not the actual deed. Your "name" is how you live and how you die in the streets. The money is the direct result of the "hustle" or the "grind" that keeps everybody fed, as the saying goes on the streets.

On July 4th weekend of 2020, 75 individuals got shot in Chicago alone. On the outside looking in we may think that gangs are at war. I'm willing to bet a penny to a nickel that isn't the problem. As I've stated many times before, old fixes to today's problems will not work any longer. Cities do have gang problems, but not the ones that they think.

First, these cities have to admit that they have issues and need assistance other than the same old worn out, tired plans, modules, interventions, preventions, treatments, programs, and interactions. Our neighborhoods and communities are going to continue to have problems, and they will only get worse and more complicated to deal with the more the folks in charge ignore their existence through effectively not trying to fix them directly. We cannot fix a foundation with a repair simply because all repairs are temporary. However, we must tear down the entire structure and start over.

Solutions at times do not require a fix. They are loud and clear and require a total makeover and rebuild, which making sense tells us that when we do rebuild, we rebuild from within for strength. In doing so that means that we must go about it a different way using different tools.

I believe that in order for any problems to be solved or fixed that an individual, company, family, organization, and/or government must look to answers by first starting with an internal look. We do effective problem-solving from the inside out, for when an issue is near, it becomes personal. We have to, whether we want to or not, look in the mirror for answers simply because in that mirror lies reality.

Let me be clear, the mirror is the reality that we look into, and if we never look into that mirror, we will never get to see the imperfections of spots, pimples, wrinkles, and worry lines that are visible. Many of us never want to look into that mirror simply because that mirror of reality exposes our imperfections and exposes who we really are.

I believe that once we do look into that mirror of reality that we will begin to understand the imperfections of others (imperfections in life). We will begin to understand the wrinkles and worry lines (problems in their lives) even more so because through that mirror we've had the opportunity to know that they exist and are very real. We have to fix and work on our own image first. After we accept the truth that we do have issues, then and only then can we help others with their own problems.

The point being that in order for us to both recognize and deal with realism we have to look for answers from within ourselves. However, we absolutely cannot see ourselves until we do look into that mirror, and we must be mature enough to accept and be willing to accept who and what is staring back at us in that mirror. This is the only way that we are going to be successful in dealing with our own realities and dealing with universal realities as well. They go hand in hand for the simple reason of we are the human race, therefore humankind's existence intertwines like a rope, making all of our issues, problems, so forth, all the same. Racism and social injustice therefore are issues of humankind, not just an African American issue. See, if an Asian person, white person, Hispanic person, or Middle Eastern person looks into that mirror I truly believe that they all will not see a perfect human being staring back at them. No one is perfect. I am convinced however that because of this truth that every human being should try to be the best man or woman that they possibly can be according to truth and reality.

Truth is God. Reality is His voice. God's voice is His word. His word is the Holy Bible. The Bible isn't just about God, it is from God. I also believe that in the imperfect problems and issues that we go through in life that God does supply us with the perfect solutions. It is up to us to embrace them and utilize those answers and solutions.

I've discovered that we at times within our humankind thinking don't adhere to nor do we embrace help, assistance, or solutions when they seem not in line with old traditional thinking and in old ways of doing things. We must know that in dealing with God that he blesses us according to how He chooses.

2 Kings 3:17, when the Israel king made war with the Moabites, coming together with the kings of Judah and Edom, they traveled for seven days into a valley without water. All the lakes were dry. The kings consulted with the prophet Elisha who told them that God said that He would provide water for them, their horses, and livestock without making it rain. See, rain is the conventional, orthodox way of water being supplied to the earth from the sky above. In our lives through most of times we are accustomed to solutions and answers being supplied to us in certain ways. I believe that the ultimate goals are solutions, period. Therefore, how God delivers them shouldn't be of a big concern. When thirsty in the middle of the desert, a chest of gold means absolutely nothing, it is worthless.

I believe that steps in moving forward are gradual steps simply because the path toward legitimacy within a society that we haven't been relevant in are always interrupted with foolishness and chaos in the ways of racism, social injustices, and inequality. The bright spot however is that although gradual steps forward are being taken, all the way from Shirley Chisholm being the first African American member of Congress in 1968, to Madeline Sweale being the first African American fighter pilot in the US Navy in 2020, I believe that things are without a doubt moving in the right direction on many things.

Everyone does, in fact, have a beginning and starting point. History in itself has a beginning. It is called the creation. I am convinced that African American people in general have the strength and determination to succeed even further, and we will. I believe that the playing field of reality and the mindset of the new millennial has demanded that we all share the same stage of life through multiracial protest, through voices that are shouting unity, through an invisible faith that is producing visible results of action that is indicating that things must change. We are saying with one unified voice, "Turn the water off, enough is enough."

It is obvious that we are in an immediate state of chaos at this point in time with the pandemic running wild and out of control. Racial tension is at an all-time high. The government has lost the confidence of the people. Certain factions are using these sensitive issues to further their own selfish agendas and messages of hate and separatism.

I am convinced that there has to be someone or someones that everyone at least respects to a certain degree or another that can intervene to say, hey, let's just hold up a minute. We need peace and understanding right now. I believe wholeheartedly that there is such an individual that can change minds, hearts, and thinking of anyone. That person is the God of Muslims, Christians, Mormons, Catholics, Episcopalians, Methodists, Baptists, Pentecostal, Nondenominational Holiness, Protestants, and Atheists alike.

In Chron. 7:14 it says, "If my people which are called by my name will humble themselves and pray, and seek my face, and turn from their wicked ways, then I will hear from heaven and will forgive their sins and heal their land." This simply means that if God's people would do just three things that God would respond in three ways: 1) That His people needed to become humble, which means to confess their sins; 2) they needed to pray, which means to repent; and 3) they needed to turn, which means to come back to him. If they did these three things then He would hear, forgive, and heal them.

Moving forward is not just something that is done physically. Moving forward has to be a state of mind, a state of conscious thought. It has to be ingrained within our hearts, minds, and souls simply because the convictions of a purpose all begin and take on action when it is on the inside of us. We as a nation of people have to believe that moving forward is the switch that turns on the process of true change. We can't move forward if we do not or refuse to accept that the old ways of thinking and the old ways of doing things in America are dangerous to our very existence. If old ways of doing things worked now in this age there wouldn't be a need for protest. We could lock arms and sing Kumbaya, march down the street in demonstration, go our separate ways, and still nothing would change or be done. Thank God this isn't that era anymore.

The most important aspect about that is that the people in charge now know that the old remedies, solutions, and tired, worn-out ways of doing business are no longer acceptable as fixes any longer. To be honest, I don't believe that many of these so-called fixes were meant to be solutions in the first place. I am convinced that they were meant to be mental mind games that the people in charge played with Black folk and the American public so that African American people could continue to be spoon fed to keep quiet (in our place).

Going forward is the action of mentally putting one idea, thought, plan in front of the other. Moving in the general direction of progress and productivity and toward common goals that actually do change things.

History is a vital part of who we are. As the tick-tock of life's clock continues to tick, we as well continue to evolve. History is very important for several reasons, with one of them being history is the very foundation of who we are, which translates to our identity. I am an avid believer that one cannot have a clear idea where they are going without knowing in which direction that they came from. Again, the starting point for all history is the creation. We all have had our own personal history that has both made and molded us in who we are individually. Experiences as we live life are an absolute part of that history because in the things that we witness, experience, and go through make us who we are, thus contributing to our belief system.

I myself and another guy were the first African American rent-a-car company over two decades ago in Houston, TX (1999-2004). Off of that experience I believe that my only limitation is myself. I believe that only I can undo me. My history was filled with trouble. I at one point was angry at the world. I felt entitled because I was an athlete used to having things my way. People praised me and turned the other way when I would act out. It took me a very long time to get it together, so to speak, but I did. I had to figure out that no one owed me anything. However, I owed myself everything.

When I received by ThD from GMOR Theology Institute it was the most joyous moment of my life. I thank God for allowing me that life experience. That experience is one of the reasons that I can put pencil to paper now and express how I feel more accurately. Everyone's life is a book, a movie, or series of some sort. We the people from every walk of life, from every nationality, creed, color, and background, form the very foundation of what America looks like. Not just one race of folk, not just one color of people, but everyone. Because you don't look like me is no longer acceptable as a crutch for racial and social inequality.

In America now one voice is heard simply because it is synchronized like a swim team ballet with others with the same like mind and the same intentions of equality, justice, fairness, and opportunity. Our voices give our agendas credibility in unison, for in our many voices of Black, white, brown, yellow, etc. there is no hope, change, strength, determination, and action. See, I found out long ago that a made-up mind cannot be stopped. Imagine thousands or millions of people with made-up minds. History is ours to make.

I believe that in a country of rights and free will that we as citizens should reserve the rights to live our lives as we so choose as long as it isn't, 1) obviously disrespecting the next person, 2) mentally or physically harming anyone, and 3) breaking the law.

I had seen a piece on the news one day that said that people were protesting because some governors ordered the citizens of their respective states to wear masks over their faces. I believe that when anything is for our good and health, both for yourself and others, that it just makes sense to comply. Whether we want to accept it or not, we are our brothers' and sisters' keepers. I guarantee that this movement of today is very different from all others that we've seen in the past. We must understand that making sense is uniquely different than common sense simply because common sense isn't really common, however, making sense only requires rational thought. In most cases all we have to do as human beings is activate that process.

My granny (RIH) used to tell us to use our heads for more than a hat stand. Making sense goes back to the analogy that I used earlier on in the book about if a person doesn't want to get sunburned, don't go out in the sun. If a person doesn't want to die in an airplane crash, simply don't board a plane. These ways of thought make sense. In order to survive, our ways of doing business as well as our solutions to these things have to make sense. All solutions aren't complicated. I do believe that in the solutions that they must coincide and coexist with the thinking and ways of life that fits a society that we are in now simply because the America Now problem-solving module is on a much different level and plain as was yesteryear in America's past. In this millennium what we see we believe, and what we hear we receive. That makes sense for sure.

In the neighborhood when someone or something is the real deal or authentic, we call them or it "the truth." The COVID-19 is real and has qualified itself as the truth. It is attacking people at an alarming rate. What is so scary about this is as the seconds, minutes, hours, days, weeks, and months add up, so do the casualties from this horrific enemy. People are getting sick at the speed of sound. I believe that we as a country have been so accustomed to dealing with any threat to our country in certain ways that we felt that we could control anything that tried to compromise the safety and security of the United States. News flash: COVID-19 didn't get the memo that there were rules to war.

We got comfortable in crisis management. We felt like we could manage from and on the same level as maybe past crises. Of course, that didn't happen. This is the time for genuine, real leadership to step forward and insert their will in order that we may at least feel some rays of hope. We need someone to take the wheel and navigate the country. Honesty has to be implemented ASAP and lead. It doesn't matter if they are Black, white, brown, or green. America needs balance right now.

This virus has also tipped the scales of harmony, which as contributed to even more chaos. Sort of like what I spoke about before about what happens when two jackals mate. Chaos plus chaos equals chaos. Someone, or someones, has to give in to what is for the good of the people. Political affiliations and political agendas are not acceptable. We the people don't care about which political party guides us through this madness. We won't forget at the polls, however. All of the grandstanding and political gerrymandering is not what's going to make us pay attention to true leadership. But when we can see out in the front of us a clear path to hope without all of the sleight of hand tricks, stage props, and outright divisions, then will we know that true leadership is all about needing someone to strike a match and light a candle in a room full of darkness. The room is beautifully furnished with elegant paintings on the walls. If there is no light in the room, it's just another dark room and no one can enjoy the beauty within.

I am a believer that effective leadership is not always directed from the front of the battle line. I look at it this way: If he or she leads from the rear, he or she doesn't expose themselves to the enemy. Also, leading from the rear gives the leader the opportunity to see everything that is out in the front of them. Also, when leading from the rear the leader isn't the primary focus of the battle. The enemy will know that they have a lot of people to go through in order to get to the leader. They have to go through the army first.

In saying a true leader doesn't want all the focus on themselves, the object of the war is the most important thing, and when a people are committed to a cause, especially in defeating an enemy of such deadly proportions, nothing can stop a determined army (society). I am certain that we will defeat this virus. I also believe that we have to defeat it as one army. Everyone has to do their part, which means listening to the experts in the field.

I believe that the Centers for Disease Control and Prevention are sincere without political agenda. I am convinced that we must listen to the people that have never lied to us before. These are the folks that have earned America's trust simply because they've proven to us that we can trust them. We as humans tend to always hold on to the glimmer of hope that someone is telling us the truth about an important issue because the humanistic side of us believes, or wants to believe, in the moral good of others. I get it.

I believe that in a crisis such as this that we have to first make sense of what it is as a society that we are dealing with, which is fairly easy to figure out for the simple fact we see the destruction and death in its path. COVID-19 is a deadly, destructive enemy of the world that has taken its toll on millions worldwide that has killed thousands on top of thousands here in the United States alone. Yet, some of us absolutely refuse to take the proper precautions to keep our families, ourselves, and others safe. We still want to party at the beaches, clubs, bars, and private parties. I believe that people take for granted this unseen enemy which has spread very seen catastrophe until it strikes near us.

The word of God says, "Warning comes before destruction." When it doesn't happen to us directly, that is the warning. Let me be clear when I say that doing things that make sense and practicing behaviors that make sense will most of the time get us through certain crises. It is an intervention strategy that we all should take heed to--safety as a prevention and intervention method in the way of masks, social distancing, and in the continuous washing of hands. Making sense in this way is safe, healthy, and responsible.

In our thinking we have to give in to what makes sense, not just for ourselves, but for everyone around us. The coronavirus is an alien enemy that is the enemy of Blacks, whites, Hispanics, indigenous, Asians, and has made it perfectly clear it is the enemy of all humankind. Matters of skin color, social status, financial status, bloodlines, political affiliation, age, neighborhood, education, and background is of no significance to this virus. This is why I am convinced that one of the primary interventions for this deadly virus is for us to be in make-sense mode at all times.

PART 3

MAKING SENSE 2

These modern-day plantations (prisons), especially in the deep South (the Confederacy) are now being manned by Africans that have arrived here from the continent of Africa in the United States on visitor, work, student, and standard visa-related protocols. Some may be here by asylum pretense as well as those who have obtained their legal permanent residency (LPR). These people arrive here from Ghana, Nigeria, Sudan, Somalia, from all over Africa for various reasons. One would assume that people from other countries do flee their countries of birth and national origin to come to the United States because these people want to upgrade their past, present, and future circumstances.

I do believe that environmental manipulation is in fact an effective tool in the toolbox of positive growth, and we can only grow when we mentally adapt and recognize that we do need certain tools to fix certain problems. Believe it or not, there is a general starting point to all fixes, and that is the act of recognizing that a problem does indeed exist. After all, how can one fix something that isn't recognized as broken?

Let me be clear, I don't frown on anyone that aspires to improve their standards of living. My issues arise when someone's aspirations disrespect others' struggles and directly supports the heinous history of many, many racial injustices, including some of the most horrific, vile acts known to humankind. The standard of living of African people, especially in the South (Confederacy), is to secure employment with the plantation (prison). They (the system) conveniently gives them authority over American slaves with titles such as parole officers, correctional officers, probation officers, and wardens. These people graciously accept these positions (thank you, massa) in the system, on these plantations, and insert themselves as not only modern-day advocates of Jim Crow law, but as gatekeepers of it to assist in slavery remaining relevant.

The Texas penal institutions are primarily populated with African American men and women statistically more than any other race of people. Parole and probation are like jobs to where people of color clock in all day, every day, and are monitored even more so. The insult is in the hiring of mostly Africans that migrated from Africa to act as honorary gatekeepers and slave managers to assist in the process of making sure that the American slave markets are up and running well in the United States of America. This is radically disrespectful, to say the least. To be honest, it poses a real, live threat to the survival of empathy, peace, and accountability.

Not only did the aggressive hiring of these people turn the pages of slavery back into the racist time warp of the 1800s, but this blatant disrespect has regressed back to a time when slaves were brought to America, and if they met the qualifications they were assigned to work in the "BIG HOUSE," which meant that they lorded over and supervised as they gave "the massa's" instructions to the common peon slaves (the field Negroes). The Big House slaves were what was considered as house Negroes. The immigrant African men and women in this era now volunteer to come to America. They volunteer to work in the slave market consisting of plantations and systematic Jim Crow DNA. (Isn't it something when the foundation of our belief system crumbles and falls down when we are yet in the building?)

The system of racial injustice and social injustice allow these African people to lord over and supervise of American Black folks, which directly says that modern-day slavery is a physical and mental reminder of a history that we really haven't overcome nor surpassed. I am convinced that because the African immigrant is from another country that they are unable to identify with the African American evolution from one fundamental phase of progression to the next simply because in a country of constantly changing rights and privileges, we as a race of people have been in a continuous cycle of progression. After all, the history books speak for themselves. An entire war was fought over the rights to own Black people as property.

Let me clear when I say it isn't that the immigrant cannot identify with our Blackness. We look alike, for sure. Two very distinct things stand out, however. Number one, everyone of the same color isn't the same kind. Number two and perhaps more importantly, the immigrant African cannot identify with our struggles here in America. If they could or did there is no way that they would be flooding the slavery market with the offers of their services for hire.

Let me also be clear when I say that I don't feel like there are comparisons to some of the things such as poverty, corrupt government, and human rights violations going on in the countries of Africa as opposed to a lot of our own struggles here in America. I am not comparing. What I am saying though is that everyone's bottom is different. America is appropriately dubbed the land of opportunity for a reason. People come here to experience a better life. I get it. However, I am convinced also that America is quietly attempting to whisper its racist rhetoric to the American Negro through the consistent hiring practices of these people, "what it means to be gracious, humble, and thankful."

Simply put, in the 1970s and a portion of the 1980s we were content with good jobs and in the privilege to both take and support our families with the income that we made. Therefore, there wasn't any need to put us back into our places. Racial segregation still existed in the '80s and a lot of life's many conveniences were still tagged as white things (golf), Black things (driving Cadillacs), and Mexican things (driving low riders). In this era some of those things have changed, and I believe that stereotypes are far and few between. My point is that the mentality has evolved of society. To sell the rights to our dignity and respect isn't an option. We must stand up in this millennial and loudly and clearly proclaim that our identity isn't for sale.

This country is built on the strongest economy in the world. Economics, hands down, is the rule. In order for any society to flourish their economic system has to be strong enough to carry the load of a society that is going to benefits its inhabitants as it becomes the epitome of all other global economic systems on the planet. I have witnessed firsthand in the United States the precedent of the economy taking first obligation over everything, even human life. The COVID-19 pandemic was and is the number one prime example.

I was taught that the obvious path to riches and success of any product is the demand of that product, and for that product is only successful when it can be supplied (demand and supply). The demand for slave labor is at an all-time high and it has been for a long, long, time in America. If a person isn't plugged into the system in some sort of way, then they will never know exactly how certain things work. The machine of legal slavery has to incarcerate and enslave members of society. They have to create laws and legislation that tends to give disadvantages to the poor and indigent citizens.

Toward a particular level in society in order that mainly over-the-top punitive actions may be enforced so that members of particular communities can keep up with the cycle of incarceration. The demand for slave labor is high because, like when cotton was the primary crop which made it the number one source toward wealth in the South, slave labor is what planted, picked, and harvested that cotton on plantations. As the times evolved, so did the intangibles because the system of slavery did learn from its mistakes (the Civil War). Therefore, the good ol' boys came up with another idea that didn't rely on one primary source of revenue because there was one thing surely not to change. The real commodity, which wasn't cotton, never has been, the number one commodity then and now has always been slaves.

The sweat shops in Asia and the products that they produce are not what is the number one commodity, but the people that work in those shops are. As in America, on those plantations that house mattress factories, tag plants (license plates), garment factories, these plants and industries produce, manufacture, and sell goods to government, private, and other state agencies throughout the country. In some states, not one slave has gotten paid one wooden nickel for being employed at any of these places and sweat shops that have profited and continue to profit each day to where they absolutely work for free.

The plantation hierarchy says that the slave's incentive for their labor is rewarded with what is called good time (the biggest con job of the century). Good time is supposed to be equivalent to the monetary compensation for slave labor. This system is intentionally illusional and is the intentional façade by the states that incorporate this system as procedure and policy. Good time is given to everyone that qualifies for it in a certain class and status depending on numerous institutional factors. However, depending on what type of offense one has, good time is purely Monopoly money. It cannot be spent nor utilized. Thus, the slave doesn't even get the chance to share crop. They work on those plantations for absolutely free, a definite human rights violation for sure.

We sometimes don't pay attention to certain things that don't concern us. Some issues have voices, meaning some politicians, influential people, and celebrities take up a cause for various reasons which does reflect action and change.

I once heard a famous politician say that education was the

essential key to not committing crime and not going to prison. "White collar" crime is committed by some of the wealthiest and most intellectually sound individuals on planet earth. I truly believe that experience is one of the most sound educations that anyone can receive. If I give a person a meal to eat, then I have fed that person for a day. If I, however, teach that person how to work for future meals, I have in turn fed them for life. In saying that, particular politicians' ways of thinking is a big part of America's not-so-correct perception of solutions to certain problems.

Education means more programs (in which most don't work), which in turn means more grants and federal money being handed out, which leads to guess what? Need I say more. In the long run it all boils down to money, and who is crafty like an ol' fox to find inventive ways to get it? Let's put it this way—many a lawyer, doctor, educational professional, corporate CEO, national ranking members of the most prestigious establishments, have been, quite frankly, locked up.

Education isn't a cure. Education is a tool in the proverbial toolbox of positive growth. The key to that toolbox is and has been systematic change. In order for the judicial system (slave auctions) to change its way of doing business, the standards in which America's outdated Jim Crow mindset of laws has to not only change, but they must be totally eradicated.

The only way that racial and social injustice will even be altered is if the American legal system of modern day slavery, which is directly supported by the United States Constitution that doesn't abolish slavery, is absolutely extinguished. Racial and social injustice are products of evil intent, greed, entitlement, racism, and ignorance.

I have always heard that all action begins with a thought. We at times base our opinions and actions from those opinions off of what is trending or seems to be the most popular. True, genuine change comes from somewhere deep down on the inside of us. Put it like this: If all of my glow came off of someone else's moonlight, what happens when that person goes somewhere else? We produce our own answers by being real to ourselves. I have often heard as well that our conscience should be our guide to right choices. True because the conscience is molded and put together by a moralistic system of what we individually and as a society deem as right or wrong. I believe that our conscience is also comprised of mental and emotional video tapes of past and present experiences of events involving conduct of moral, ethical, and standardized turpitude.

Let me be clear, right and wrong isn't dictated by a set of circumstances. Right and wrong is defined by God and violated by mankind, which means that the choice to do either lays eternally at the very foundation of both who we are and to whom we aspire to become, giving us in turn the power to act on how we feel through exactly what we believe in.

We absolutely cannot fear good decisions, nor can we fear sensible choices. Personally, everything that I fear has already happened to me. I believe that before a slave is freed back into society, especially after being in captivity for possibly decades, that he or she be prepared to go back into society so that he or she can have a legitimate opportunity to succeed. They need to go through a rigorous, in-depth, laced-with-reality reentry program, not these basic standard (one-size-fits-all) programs that focus on make-believe expectations and false hope. This is one of the primary areas that the system fails in so-called rehabilitation initiatives. They scratch their heads at recidivism and violent crime. The very key to keeping recidivism down is in the prep before they are set free on the streets of America.

Think about this: the last lesson of goodwill is what mostly inspires and motivates the first acts of humility once allowed back into society. Every act of humankind derives from what they know to do. Everyone is different therefore we all are very different in character, thus a difference in our issues and needs as well. Number one, those needs must be met. Number two, those issues must be confronted and dealt with. Incarceration does neither. Incarceration locks away issues and needs while often preserving them (keeping them on ice) and creating even more dangerous other issues and needs.

So, guess what happens when a person is freed after not having had any help dealing with these things? Scary, huh? The most important phase of reentry should center around individuality. Why? Because everyone should have their own personalized, individual reentry plan. Not just the titled "Individualized," but an actual plan that fits the individual's profile, history, etc. These programs should be taught by people that have been successful participants of the reentry program in certain phases that are accomplished. Some people can't change their negative, destructive thinking patterns because they don't know how. In the real world we know that the business (literally) of incarceration takes precedent over all else. Why would the system teach a slave how to not come back and work for free?

There is such a thing as inherited poverty. We change this predicament once we transition into adulthood and we get uncomfortable with being broke. This millennial has become uncomfortable with the way America has been doing business and this is what the multi-racial protests are saying to the world. We have a lot of work to do as a country. I have heard it said that the recidivism in America is low and that most crime is down (except homicide). These often-maligned statistics and political propaganda are directly the roots of our problems like I wrote about earlier in this book concerning the magic trick of sleight of hand (everything that you see isn't really real because it's an illusion). It's not as though recidivism is down as much as it is about at one time the system was on a roll at issuing out lengthy sentences, therefore recidivism started decreasing because people never got out to reoffend. In retrospect, the system handed out small sentences to younger offenders and this trend increased the numbers that were on probation or parole.

Hypothetical question: What would happen if all of this would just stop, meaning, if modern day slavery was just POOF, gone? Think about the financial implications, how much revenue, investment, business (old TV game show host) would stand to lose. This is why, or one of the reasons why, slavery in these times is necessary and a force within the United States. Not to lock up bad people (Capitol Hill is a perfect example), but to keep and maintain business interests. Allow me to reiterate that COVID-19 clearly showed everyone in broad, open daylight for all to lay witness to that the ECONOMY of these United States of America is King, master, and ruler. Human life takes an immediate backseat to it, hands down.

I believe in what I call, "making sense solutions." I also believe that these solutions that there are or is one key element that is the example of true change and real difference-making. The first thing is there has to be a clear, absolute agreement that a change and a different direction of the journey needs to take place. Maybe the most important aspect of change is constructive communication. Perfect example, if I step on your toe and you never say ouch or make me aware that I stepped on your toe I'll never have the opportunity to acknowledge my fault and apologize for it. We have to be willing and able to come and sit down at the table of communication listening, being empathetic, understanding, and the table of making sense, for in these things change, hope, and constructive evolving of society is inevitable. My ideas and my opinions are valid, as are yours as long as they don't demean or harm anyone else. I don't have to like them, nor do I have to agree with them, but I must acknowledge their validity.

I believe that people of all races, creeds, origins, and nationalities have come together and have forged a bond of common unity simply because this is their voice of one people. Because you don't look like me doesn't mean that you don't think like me. Because you don't look like me doesn't mean that our eyes don't see the same things or that our ears don't hear the same chaos. A lot of times controversies and issues bond folks together like never before. Racial and social injustices have been around for a long while and have had issues for even longer, until recent times. However, these things have not been the main issues. Injustices have not taken center stage as it has in modern times simply because the platform hasn't been as accessible as it is now in the 21st Century.

I heard the other day and confirmed it that the lawyers for one of the police officers charged in George Floyd's murder was attempting to get the charges thrown out of court due to the fact that Mr. Floyd was alleged to have illegal drugs in his system at the time of his arrest and murder.

10, 9, 8, 7, 6, 5, 4, 3, 2, 1, 0.

Okay. First and foremost, drugs didn't use excessive force and wrestle George Floyd to the ground. The police did.

Drugs didn't keep its knee on George Floyd's neck for eight minutes and 46 seconds, cutting off his life's oxygen supply. The police did. When George Floyd uttered the now-famous phrase, "I can't breathe," it wasn't drugs talking. It was a man, a father, a son, a brother, a human being whose very life at that moment was being choked out of him by the officers of the Minneapolis Police Department.

This is what transpires when a system made to protect people from bad things happening to them have amongst them bad people that are only concerned with violence, aggression, force, authoritarian ideologies, and with only protecting themselves. This is the very core of the issues with many police departments all across America. I say take your per se "lick" and try to rebuild your life, pray for forgiveness (murder), and move forward as you may.

Of course, it is always easier said than done, and truthfully it won't be easy at all. Reality says that inevitably all of us must answer for our wrongs and indiscretions, some of us sooner than later. Point being, a power greater than any ultimately judges all in the end.

I stated about a few bad apples earlier, which is true. What occurs when a few of those bad apples are integrated into a systemic rotation then trained, nurtured, and cultivated within a culture of likeminded folk, tragedies such as what happened to George Floyd and many like him occurs. The system doesn't get a pass by any means, meaning for so long these officers are trained to conduct themselves in a certain way during certain situations.

I am quite sure that these are but a couple of reasons that they are entrusted with human wellbeing and human life. Police are specifically trained to handle adverse, aggressive, and diverse instances. In these particular situations (George Floyd and others), not only did police fail to protect human wellbeing, trust, service, and the preservation of human life, but the system in which they were trained is as guilty if not even more so simply because if the education and training that they had received had been employed as counteractions or as deterrents to what actually did occur during this senseless murder of George Floyd, then truthfully Mr. Floyd would be alive today.

It is safe to say, then, that these particular police officers' training and their own recorded actions are primary reasons that we are at the point that we are today. These police officers reflected through violence and aggression who they were conditioned to be. They, the police officers of their respective police departments, acted according to how they were trained to both act and react. Therefore, these police officers' actions and conduct reflected protocol. The accountability of the entire police department in Minneapolis, Minnesota should also be on trial.

As I stated earlier on in this book, there are two distinct definitions of law. The first is what a law actually means. A law is a standard of conduct. It is a rule that forms part of the law. The law is a system of laws. This system is made up of rules and principles that govern society in which not even a king is above. These rules and principles form a unified system of guidance and order for conduct. In this not only were many laws broken and violated, but the law was obstructed, defiled, and ignored. In a functional democratic society of laws, when they are violated there are consequences. The consequences of violating these laws by the police officers will be a trial in a court of law to determine the truth.

It really doesn't matter at this point what anyone else believes (not even myself). Only the individuals on the inside will take center stage for the entire world to lay witness to. I pray that in this process that truth does prevail simply because where there is truth there is fundamental justice void of just us.

I believe that at times when humankind is attempting to have their opinions, agendas, and beliefs championed that the truth often gets distorted with personal distractions because in these moments the truth is no longer the primary goal, winning is, sometimes at all costs. We as humankind more often than not will say anything and play tricks with our own minds just so that we can say that we were right. By being an actual student of law, I personally can relate to the win as the ultimate goal simply because winning projects and mirrors success.

Let me be clear, the truth is the only thing that is definite. I believe that the truth is the only thing that makes us all as a society pay very close attention to our misconceptions of certain things. We know that from certain experiences that a lot of times we as humankind would rather believe in untruths. Why? Because this is where many people are comfortable in being. This state of being becomes their comfort zone. I believe that dealing with reality doesn't feel too good at times. More times than not it exposes our weaknesses. I think by exposing those weaknesses this makes many of us feel vulnerable. No one likes feeling this way.

We must realize that life comes full circle. It always does. Truth (reality) is a tenacious hunter, it will always find us. I always use the analogy of when the dead is buried. We put someone in the ground only to return during our lifetime to repeat this process over and over again, at least until it's our time to be left behind. I have heard it said by others that individual truths are a reality. That what may be true for one person may not exactly be the truth for another. This is part of why chaos is rampant and confusion is at an all-time high. Examples of general truths: Someone in the world was born today; likewise, someone died today. General absolute, undisputed truths.

I believe that there isn't a legal system that can clearly be defined or explained on mere logical terms. Our legal system was born in the Anglo-Saxon period, which transitioned into Anglo-American. Mostly we are governed under what is called the common law, which is simply supposed to punish wrong and maintain peace and order according to the law. Since this way is supposed to be the standard in which a functional body of folks are supposed to be living in, what happens when that standard is violated by the very institution that has sworn to protect and serve the body of people that it violated? The trust in the establishment is damaged severely, which creates a culture of dysfunction. Not very far behind dysfunction is its cousin, chaos.

How is trust regained? Definitely not in the same way that it was lost. Albert Einstein once said that problems can't be solved with the same mindset that created them. The bare bones of the matter is that the system of slavery has to turn into a judicial system. The slave auctions have to turn into true courtrooms of law that are intended for everyone no matter their financial, social, or political status and/or affiliations. The slave plantations that are disguised as prisons must institute rehabilitation as a first response instead of enjoying the fruits of free labor. The police departments nationwide not only have to coexist with its various communities, but they must be involved with their community's infrastructure. Thus, they'll know what is needed to grow, nurture, build, and to keep safe that particular community.

They (police) must know that the very key to doing these things within the community is trust. The local hierarchy of government (city hall) must establish multiculturalism as essential in order that folks of every race, creed, color, national origin, and indigenous within the same municipality can flourish, grow, build, and succeed together as one society. The state governments have to change the way that they do business as well. Let's put it this way, political agendas have been around for a long, long time, and I believe that they will continue to be around for even longer.

My thought is if only but a few of the legislators would just simply change politics, a lot of good things can come from positive change. I believe that nationally a party affiliation is one of the main Achilles' heels to honest, ethical governance in the United States. Donkeys aren't always right. Neither are elephants.

The number one greatest attribute that humankind can have both externally and internally is God. I am convinced that one's character and conscience is the staple of who they are. Through both of these things we should discover a lot about ourselves and others as well. Decisions in governance is most definitely about the character of the Congress person or Senator. See, party affiliation simply means a common interest of ideology, not a likeness in character, which should be shaped by morals, ethics, experiences, standards, and fundamental truths. No man or woman that believes in truth can look at or hear an untruth and declare it righteous in the name of common interest.

Idealism…shame on you. Perfection isn't afforded to anyone. We as a people under one God must give in to what keeps us unified. We must make this society better. We can do that by loving one another in spite of. We as the human race must rise up as one to push back against those that choose to spread messages of hate, separatism, division, supremist rhetoric, entitlement, inequality, and racial and social injustice.

Believe this: This movement of America Now is most definitely BIGGER than their message. The old ways of doing business in America have to be redirected to meet the concerns, needs, and ideas that identify with the society of today. We have to use the tools that are afforded to us in the toolbox of positive growth so that we may succeed as a race of people that are certainly focused on true growth and true change that we all can believe in.

My greatest motivation was witnessing the celebrations of my failures. To succeed, we must be of one mind, one movement. This millennium is about new fresh ideas, new air, new fresh energy. This era isn't about because you look like me, but it is about because you think like me, you feel like me, you love like me, and because we are all one in these same things. That means that you believe like me in equality, in racial and social justice, in this way of believing that bonds us to a society of good and bad. Togetherness is what this is ultimately all about.

In the end, Black or white, brown or yellow, liberal or progressive, conservative, or moderate, there has to be a willingness and it all boils down to the meeting of all people so that they may coexist as one society.

I don't profess to have all of the answers. Then too, there are or may not be any clear-cut remedies to our nation's woes. I have often heard that it is next to impossible to fight fire with fire, at least until I saw it done, meaning that I truly believe that in order to gain a true path to real change in anything that at times we have to embrace often nontraditional solutions to fix today's issues and problems.

We as a society are going to sink lower into a pit of despair, division, and desperation, and we are going to lose valuable ground in creating solutions as old problems continue to resurface in the new age of people that cannot relate nor identify with problem-solving of old. This is why they push both back and against so-called authority and authoritarian attitudes of police. Politicians talking about kick the can as an entertainment outlet for kids of today, murder as a solution for not abiding by police commands, the military walking the community streets of our country, an unknown virus that started killing people without warning. This America pushes against the things that they cannot relate to that make them feel uncomfortable, and racism is probably at the top of that list.

I read somewhere a few weeks ago that a music and entertainment star returned a Ferrari sports car back to the dealership in which he purchased it from because he couldn't figure how to start it up. The society of today is pretty much like this star in that traditional ways of doing things are unfamiliar to them. It makes them unsure, uncomfortable, inadequate, simply because that particular avenue may be foreign to them. They can't turn the car on, so to speak (utilize it), to be of any use to them. The old way was to figure it out, but not today. In this society they simply find another source (get a car that we can start).

I believe when we exercise our resources we build strength in allies, relations, creativity, and idealism. I believe that these things are put into motion because this millennial refuses to sit still and accept anything as a remedy. New tools, revisions, and upgraded versions have to be manufactured to meet the needs of the America Now society.

In conclusion, we all must come to both recognize and understand that real peace isn't the absence of noise or discord, but real peace is the absolute presence of ORDER.

ABOUT THE AUTHOR

Dr. T.K. Harvey-Allen graduated from GMOR (Gospel Ministry Outreach Institute of Theology) in 2015 in Houston, Texas under the divine teaching and direction of Dr. E.D. Thronton. Dr. Harvey-Allen was at a stagnate state in his life. At that particular time in his life he was married, financially stable, and had added another degree to his resume; yet at that time in his life still didn't have a clue even though his life seemed to be okay from the outside looking in. After receiving his T.hd from GMOR, Dr. Harvey-Allen assumed as did everyone else that he would go on to preach the gospel, following in the anointed footsteps of his father. He soon discovered that the ministry of that nature wasn't his true calling. Along the way, however, Dr. Harvey-Allen made it his business to soak up every bit of knowledge pertaining to theology that he could. Dr. Merdice Brown soon became one of his most trusted sources about theology and life in general. The problem was that here he had a T.hd and didn't know what to do with it. Year four out of the theology institute is is believed that divine intervention prevailed. Dr. Harvey-Allen once said that he truly didn't understand until he acted as King Hezekiah did (2 Kings 20.1-11) and turned to the wall and had a one-on-one with God. Dr. Harvey-Allen's call came to him, that calling as a theologian is to teach and enlighten through the creative writing of books and study material. Pencil and paper is the stage of stories untold, truths never revealed, and from perspectives without fear. Dr. Harvey-Allen engages with his readers as he feels guided in spirit and the footsteps of the divine, this book as others that he has authored in where those footsteps have led him thus far. We pray that you enjoy. Most of all, we pray that you are enlightened.

www.ingramcontent.com/pod-product-compliance
Lightning Source LLC
Chambersburg PA
CBHW071904070526
44583CB00016B/1836